WATER
SNOW
WATER

WATER
SNOW
WATER

Constructive Living
for Mental Health

David K. Reynolds, PhD

UNIVERSITY OF HAWAI'I PRESS

Honolulu

Library of Congress Cataloging-in-Publication Data

Reynolds, David K., author.
Water, snow, water : constructive living for mental
health / David K. Reynolds, Ph. D.
pages cm
Includes bibliographical references.
ISBN 978-0-8248-3695-5 (pbk. : alk. paper)
1. Morita psychotherapy. 2. Naikan psychotherapy.
3. Conduct of life. 4. Mental health. I. Title.
RC489.M65R533 2013
616.89'14—dc23
2013008408

Designed by Julie Matsuo-Chun
Printed by Edwards Brothers Malloy

Contents

Preface

The title of this book, *Water, Snow, Water* comes from the deathbed haiku of the Japanese poet Raizan:

> Farewell.
> From water to water,
> The path of snow.

That's us, of course. Dust to dust, water to water, molecules to molecules. I am a living, breathing phase; a moving, thinking excerpt; a sensitive, vibrating chord. You too of course.

We would do well to reflect sometimes upon the larger whole of which we are animated components. How do we fit in? For what purpose have we been embedded in this flowing glacier called time? What does reality require of us? What is the benefit of having us around for these moments? I definitely will NOT ask you "How do you feel about that?"

It has taken me more than ten years, off and on, to write this book. I expected *A Handbook for Constructive Living* to be my last book about the theory and practice of Constructive Living (CL). I imagine that you may come across ideas in this book that are new to you, even contradictory to what you may have thought before. Then again, maybe not. What was novel in the last century has been recognized and relabeled to some degree over the past decade or so.

Human wisdom has depth that goes beyond cultural boundaries and temporal fashions.

Introduction

Happiness is fine. However, achieving your goals is more important than being happy. Enduring some discomfort and anxiety is worth living life with positive accomplishment. Living constructively, living a meaningful life, making a contribution to your world are more satisfying than just feeling good temporarily. If what you just read makes sense to you, then read on; this guidebook for sustaining a worthwhile life will be useful to you.

You can't be happy all the time. You can't feel comfortable all the time. You can't have the feelings you want when you want them for as long as you want them. Life just doesn't work that way. Maybe you have tried counseling, therapy, diets, meditation, chemicals, or some sort of esoteric magic to work on your feelings, to fix your life or make it perfect. Nothing has worked as well as you had hoped. Reading this book won't solve your life problems either. But it will give you some sensible, practical, and doable suggestions—suggestions about how to work on your life. The key word here is work. Sitting and talking with someone is not enough. Venting your feelings is not enough. Putting your mind in some quiet inner place is not enough. Working on your life involves moving your body, living your life purposefully and constructively. This book offers you concrete assignments for such activity.

I call this approach to life "Constructive Living" (CL). CL is about building your life on purpose and behavior. It was borrowed from two Japanese thinkers but redesigned to respond to two *un*realistic elements of modern Western culture. The first is its exclusive focus on feelings, as though feelings were the only aspect of life with meaning. Some simple-minded westerners believe that feelings must be repaired before undertaking any project. The second unrealistic element is the mistaken belief that one can succeed only through one's own efforts, that, for example, despite the deficiencies of one's parents and their improper childrearing, one can struggle and overcome such handicaps and "make it to the top" on one's own. One can become a "self-made" person.

The first fallacy ignores the element of purposeful action, which is possible to take even when feelings are unsupportive or even painful. And the second fallacy ignores the reality of the importance of the essential support of other people and things to achieving success. I suggest that you look at your past—your whole past—and put any traumatic experiences in perspective by looking at all the supportive and positive experiences that we encounter on a daily basis. Too many Americans just don't consider that right-before-your-nose reality.

We are taught that the ideal is to work hard to overcome the handicaps our parents (or others) may have laid upon us by overprotection, sexual or physical or mental abuse, lack of love, and the like. Who asks us to think about all the diapers someone changed for us as babies? Who asks us to consider all the meals cooked and dishes washed and clothes laundered for us? Who insists that we reflect on the kindness of the people who taught us and hired us and listened to our complaints about the unkindness of our world? Well, I do. And I have been insisting on looking at the larger picture of past and present for more than thirty years now, since the time I began to understand some Japanese psychotherapies that were not burdened by the narrow perspective of Western values and therapies. For years I have been asking Western clients why they persist in hanging all the clothes in the closets of their past on just one hanger—one traumatic event, one terrible experience, one destructive person. Do you know how helpless human infants are? Do you know what effort it takes to feed, cuddle, change, and keep them warm whether the parent or parent-surrogate feels like it all the time or not? Do you realize the amount of effort it takes on the part of people you've never met to get your train or plane or bus to your destination? Have you reflected on what sort of complex set of activities by countless strangers results in putting the food on your table, the clothes in your wardrobe, the newspaper or news program in your home, the car in your driveway?

You may have had one or more terrible experiences in your past. I've had some, too. But those traumas do not define your past or cripple you psychologically. Sure, you can use those experiences to give up on yourself. In America many people will console, treat you sympathetically, and forgive you almost anything if you cite the disasters of your past. It's about time Americans grew up and looked at more of reality than the simple self-serving caricatures of traumas. Life is sometimes very tough. But life in this country is much more often filled with favors received, unacknowledged, and unappreciated. When you grow tired of complaining and catharsis, check out a wider view of who you are and where you have been, what you need to do, and what has been done for you. Check out Constructive Living.

Have you ever been worried that you couldn't find anything to worry about? Have you ever worried about what to worry about next? Have you ever worried that you worry too much? Have you ever worried that you don't worry enough? Have you ever worried that worrying isn't good for your health? Worries, worries—there are endless supplies of them to the mind that can't find something better to contemplate at the moment. Anyone who advises that you just stop worrying, that you turn off your worries, has no sense of the sheer impossibility of that advice. So, while worrying, let's work on getting along with our lives.

Questions and Answers about
Constructive Living (CL)

Over the years articles about Constructive Living have appeared in *Cosmopolitan, USA Today, American Health, New Woman, Fitness, Self, "O" Magazine, Vogue, Men's Health, New Dimensions, The Japan Times, Common Ground,* and elsewhere. The *Cosmopolitan* article alone prompted inquiries from more than five thousand readers representing all fifty U.S. states and some foreign countries. The journalists who wrote those articles carefully presented a fair and positive image of this Japanese-based perspective on mental health. I begin with these interviews and queries in order to clarify some of the questions and assumptions about psychotherapy in the minds of westerners and how CL often reframes and replies to those assumptions and queries in novel ways.

Claudia Interview

This chapter is adapted from a series of questions posed by a Brazilian journalist after she read an article about CL in the March 2001 issue of *"O" Magazine.* My responses were published in the magazine *Claudia* in 2001.

What is Constructive Living?
CL is a sensible, practical educational approach to living well in the modern world.

Is it a way of life or does it work as a therapy to overcome a specific problem?

It is not therapy. CL instructors don't treat "patients." We educate students, offer homework assignments, and so forth. CL involves down-to-earth teaching. There is no stigma or lower status attached to being a student as there may be with being a patient in therapy, no assumption that the student is abnormal, in need of being "fixed." Anyone can benefit from CL study.

How can one apply CL to one's everyday life? Are there special techniques?

CL is based on doing realistic learning, assignments, and exercises. The best way to learn its principles is to do some of the assignments.

What's the basic principle of CL?

We aim to help our students become more realistic. We are all sometimes happy, sometimes not; sometimes confident, sometimes not; sometimes clever, sometimes not. It is realistic to accept ourselves as we are even while working to improve. Basic principles of the *action aspect* of CL include accepting all of reality (including your feelings) as it is, knowing your purpose, doing what needs doing.

Realistically, you cannot change your past; you must accept it. But you can change your view of the past. The reflection aspect of CL helps us to look at our past and our present from a wider perspective. We recognize how we have been and continue to be supported by others—even when we thought we were merely suffering victims.

How can we change a situation or overcome a problem when we're supposed to accept feelings as they are?

Accepting reality is the first step in making changes. People who fantasize (e.g., "If only my situation were different"; "If only I had been born to different parents"; "If only he hadn't left me.") are living in unreality. A more realistic approach is to think something like "Here is the situation; I don't like it; what can I do to change it?" That is realistic. Trying to battle with one's feelings is foolish. No one can turn feelings on and off at will.

How can people use unpleasant feelings in their favor?

Feelings give us information. That fellow makes you anxious. That woman makes you feel unworthy. You like that client. You may feel nervous before boarding an airplane. All these feelings suggest things you might do to deal with them (behavior). If you're afraid of airplanes, maybe you should check on the safety records of various airlines and choose the safest one for your flight. Maybe you should put your affairs in order before boarding a plane, just in case.

But feelings are not the only source of information in deciding what to do. Our purposes also inform us about what needs doing. There may be social factors, economic factors, legal factors, and personal preferences that need to be taken into account before going into action.

If you're downcast and troubled, how can you succeed and acquire more self-esteem?

You have been taught that you must adjust your feelings before you can do something. That order is backwards. Actually, it is doing something well and successfully that leads to self-esteem. Actions influence, even create, feelings. For example, depressed people are more likely to feel better after they've taken a walk, gotten some exercise. Trying to encourage depressed people to *feel* like taking a walk may at first be difficult or impossible. So we start with changing behavior, not with trying to work on feelings directly.

By the way, attaining high self-esteem may be neither necessary nor realistic. Sometimes I am kind, sometimes not; sometimes smart, sometimes stupid; sometimes happy, sometimes not. Why should I expect to feel good about myself all the time when I am so changeable? Sometimes I deserve self-esteem, sometimes not. Better than *self*-esteem is *reality*-esteem. Whether I am good or bad in any given moment this computer still works for me, truckers continue to deliver groceries to the supermarket for me, my heart keeps beating for me, and so forth. People and things keep taking care of me even though I keep changing. Realistically, I can esteem and respect that continuous support.

What happens to people who live by CL principles? What kind of people are they?
Just like everyone else, they keep changing. But they recognize the fact. They work on their debt to reality—to parents and spouses and life partners and children and fellow workers. They derive satisfaction from living life well, and this satisfaction occurs more and more often as they master the art of living. They are not pushed about by their feelings. They feel deeply and still do what they need to do. So they increase the likelihood of being successful in their lives. Moments of self-esteem may come more often, but CL people aren't obsessed with generating them.

I read that CL is being used in schools, jails, and hospitals. How can this educational way of life help a terminally ill person?
We all live until we die. We humans, whether school students or prisoners in jails or patients in hospitals, can all benefit from living realistically. To pretend about or deny feelings is foolish. But to let feelings rule our lives is equally foolish, and not a game one can win with any consistency, because feelings are uncontrollable directly by one's will. The dying patient who thinks only of her fear of death misses the chance to live well during the last days of her life.

Does CL have to be applied by a therapist, a teacher, or a counselor? Is it taught in a classroom?
In order to become a certified CL instructor one must take a ten-day intensive certification course. I have conducted certification training in the United States, New Zealand, Australia, Canada, and Japan (in Japanese). During that course I live alongside the trainees while teaching CL principles and giving CL assignments. The trainees are watching my everyday life and I am watching theirs. There is a morn-

ing seminar and individual sessions when assignments are given for the rest of the day. We cook and eat and study and work and play together. That is the way most of us spend a lot of the time in our lives anyway. There is a mid-term and a final exam.

Fewer than half the trainees who finish the ten days are certified immediately. Those who are not certified are given a number of years to put CL into practice and then reapply for certification. They need attend no more courses or pay more money. Certification means only that I am satisfied that they understand the basic principles of CL, that they can talk about it meaningfully to others, and that they live it to some degree in their daily lives. No one does CL perfectly, of course. Me included. But CL people, when they fail, simply turn to the next thing that needs to be done. They don't waste time beating themselves up about having made another mistake. What needs doing now?

How do you change your habits and start this new lifestyle?
Change is inevitable. Our circumstances change. We grow older. People come and go from our lives. Each moment brings fresh opportunities and challenges. There is no possibility of staying the same. So it is the kind of changing that is important. What you do affects that changing, *is* that changing.

Isn't CL good only for emotionally strong people, people with strong wills?
CL is for everyone. "For all my dreams, I am what I do" is a quote from one of the CL books. After we get our lives in some order, after we build habits of doing well, with full attention to what comes to us to do, then people say that we are strong people. You don't have to be strong to start living your life well; you just have to start living your life well. That is reassuring. Therein lies hope.

How can one overcome fears?
Fears don't need to be overcome. I fly afraid all the time. You have been taught that fears prevent you from doing something, that they

paralyze you. That is a myth. Fears should be noticed, checked for information, and accepted. Then get on with the next thing you need to do. Behavior is controllable. You are responsible for everything you do, but not responsible for anything you feel. Feelings happen to you. But what you do in life is up to you.

Western culture seems to use excuses and even drugs aimed at feeling good. What does CL have to say about that?
Many people in the world want fast cures for any discomfort. There is a price to pay for such childishness. It is natural to feel bad sometimes. What is important is to work toward your goals, to work on accomplishing your purposes whether you're feeling good or bad at the moment. That approach to life turns out to be more satisfying than seeking immediate relief from any distress.

Aren't we supposed to look for happiness no matter what?
No. Don't believe the advertising. Don't be fooled.

You say that anxiety is good and useful, why? Doesn't it paralyze people?
See my answers above. That you feel anxious before meeting a new date, for example, tells me you want to do well on the date, you want to be liked. Anxiety before an examination tells me you want to do well on the examination; people who don't care how the exam turns out are relaxed. Anxiety provides us with good information. Remember that people who cannot feel physical pain can bleed to death or further injure a broken leg because they don't experience discomfort. Discomfort is useful.

How can a person work with their anxiety, fears, and depression and still do what they have to do?
You don't need to "work with" feelings. You don't need to express them or "get them out." You just need to notice them and go on with your life. People used to believe that a person could be possessed by a

hidden devil and went to a religious professional who could identify the devil and exorcise it. Nowadays some people believe that they have hidden feelings and go to a mental health professional who can somehow perceive those feelings and bring them out in order to neutralize their power. There is no difference between the two. They are both religious beliefs, not science. If you are not feeling something you are not feeling it. There are no unconscious feelings. That is a myth started by Freudian psychoanalysis years ago.

In this case, people should fire their therapists, live with their problems, and get things done—right?
There are people who are genuinely ill. They may have some chemical imbalance in the brain. They may need medication. But medication doesn't teach people how to live well. Those people with illnesses could take their medication and also study about life from Constructive Living books or instructors. To sit and talk about one's problems for an hour a week year after year is not likely to solve many life problems. If one is in any kind of therapy there should be homework assignments involving action. Some modern therapies such as Acceptance Commitment Therapy and other behavior-based therapies with experimental roots arrive at similar techniques to the clinical-based Constructive Living.

Is that possible when you're not focused and determined? Does it work for people in crisis or who are lost in their personal and professional lives?
You have been taught that you must make a commitment, pull yourself together, empower yourself, or make a decision before you change what you do. That is not so. You may know people who are caught in the traps of trying to make themselves feel like going to work or trying to make themselves feel a deeper commitment to their work or trying to feel more determined. They believe that if they just talk to someone (in therapy, for example, or to a friend) that they are "working on themselves." That is silly. You don't need any mental preparations

before changing what you do. Just do it. When you discover this truth, not just by reading about it, but by practicing it and experiencing it, then you discover there is great freedom in your life. You don't need to get yourself "focused" or "together" or "empowered." Just do it.

When you find yourself in a crisis situation it is often useful just to simplify your behavior. Focusing on your feelings when in crisis makes you feel even more powerless and out of control, whereas focusing on behavior gives you a sense of being in control, and realistically so, because your behavior is that part of your life over which you actually have control. Lots of talk about feelings only burdens other people and makes things worse.

Common Ground interview

The following section is adapted from a *Common Ground* interview in 2000.

I understand that you developed Constructive Living based on two Japanese psychotherapies—Morita therapy and Naikan therapy. Didn't you run into resistance when introducing these Japanese ideas into the West?

Although its roots lie much deeper in human history, Constructive Living itself has only been around since 1984. It's frustrating. Just as I was getting accustomed to being a rebel in the field of mental health our ideas started to sound like mainstream therapeutic wisdom. For example, CL recommendations for dealing with depression (physical exercise and stimulus input) are common knowledge these days. Our advice on coping with panic (wait, distract yourself, engage in some activity) has even appeared in Ann Landers' column. CL's counsel on work (though it is not necessarily fun, it can be satisfying anyway, doing what we have to do is meaningful) can be found in much popular writing these days. What to do about failure (turn to the next golf shot) has been suggested in *USA Today*. What to do about trash in public places (pick it up) is echoed in the *Elmwood Newsletter* and the *Meaningful Life Therapy* newsletter. Miss Manners confirms our position that being "comfortable" has become an unhealthy ultimate value. Naikan-like reciprocity reflection and confession turn out to be good for the immune system according to Pennebaker at SMU. Larimer, in *USA Weekend,* advises those in the Recovery movement to quit blaming mothers for current ills, and Winnicott (in a Basic Books edition) suggests that we recognize mothers' contribution to society instead of vilifying them. In the *Maine Sunday Telegram* Sanford offers CL-like advice that to improve interpersonal relations it is helpful to work on changing yourself first and acting positively even when you don't feel like it. Meacham on brief therapy in *Focus* recommends that we resist labels and focus on doing. Even the television program *L.A. Law* suggests that "You learn from what you do, not from what you don't do." I have an overflowing scrapbook of cartoons from newspapers around the United States exemplifying Constructive Living principles and poking fun at outmoded stereotypical thinking in the field of mental health. Times are changing.

Constructive Living is meaningful realism. Fifteen years ago my father died. Mail still comes for him offering life insurance and medical coverage. Some current mental health advice is as outmoded as that useless mail. Westerners, especially Americans, seem to want a quick answer, simple definitions, a two-minute solution. But life is not so simple: being cautious, even being anxious is not good or bad, feelings are too complex to be explained; life must be lived out, life cannot be summed up in a paragraph. Up until the late twentieth century American readers were taught a lot of foolishness that was probably well-intentioned but destructively unrealistic. The foolishness was based on theories created by people who were not in touch with everyday life.

What are the absolutely essential elements of Constructive Living? What defines it as a unique lifeway or therapeutic method?
First let me say a few words about what is *not* essential to Constructive Living. As far as I can see, there are some characteristic techniques

but no specific techniques that are essential. We can do Constructive Living without doing absolute bedrest, as in Japan's Morita therapy, and without seated meditation, as in Japan's Naikan therapy. We can do Constructive Living without diary guidance or reading assignments, key parts of the original Japanese therapies (though we may choose to use these methods).

There is nothing particularly Japanese about Constructive Living. It isn't necessary to use foreign words like *shinkeishitsu* or *toraware*, or the names Morita and Yoshimoto. There is no requirement that our students be interested in Zen or things Japanese.

So what is left? As far as I can see, there are a few essential principles, orientations, and a small class of techniques that constitute the core of Constructive Living, or CL as we call it.

What are some of the basic principles of CL?

First let us consider the reality focus in CL. Reality must be accepted as it is. Feelings are a natural part of reality. It follows that they must be accepted, without direct struggle.

Both Morita and Naikan ask us to look at reality. And both lead us to act on reality. It isn't enough to ponder, ruminate, intellectualize, imagine. We must take what we know into the world and apply it in order to keep learning, growing, and living.

Some suffering in the world is based on real problems. Other kinds of suffering are based on excessive self-focus and experiential ignorance. The solution to the latter kinds is experience-based education. The essential goal of CL is to see reality clearly, something we haven't done because we haven't paid proper attention (Morita), have inadvertently misperceived it (Morita), or have selfishly misperceived it (Naikan).

A side effect of the Morita lifeway may be reduction in symptoms or suffering. It may take the form of a new appreciation of the colors and variety in nature. A side effect of Naikan may be gratitude, guilt, or some other feeling. It may be a resolve to repay the world or clean up one's life or sweep the sidewalk. But both therapies require us to recognize and encounter specific, concrete, detailed reality. They discourage overuse of abstraction, generalization, and vagueness.

Second, CL emphasizes the need to put what we have learned into our daily life activities. Morita and Naikan are not ways of living that ultimately remove us from the world into some nonproductive withdrawn existence. They are at their best and most useful as we operate in everyday life.

As I have said, behavior is the controllable aspect of reality. It is through purposeful, realistic behavior that we can work to change reality. We are responsible for what we do no matter what we feel. There are a few phenomena (some people include them in the category of behaviors), such as stuttering, trembling, and impotence, that are not directly controllable by the will. They are considered to be uncontrollable expressions of feelings and must be accepted as they are while the student works on controllable behaviors.

Attention must be focused on reality. Reality is the proper teacher of life's lessons. Observation of reality results in information about what needs to be done (i.e., purposeful behavior). When what needs to be done is not clear, Morita can suggest only to do what *is* clear. This is part of the reason for the structured nature of Zen monasteries. One's situation, when properly structured, presents what needs to be done in relatively routine and clear fashion so that attention can be invested in performing activities well. The simple and organized life reduces the attention necessary for deciding what needs doing.

Intellectual understanding may be helpful on some level, but action-grounded experiential understanding is more dependable and beneficial. Action based on reality teaches truth. Reflection on the past and planning for the future may provide useful insights and valuable preparations, but excessive rumination and daydreaming are self-centered and harmful.

There is something about action, the moment of acting, that frees us from thoughts, fixations, and unrealistic concerns. Of course we need to plan for the future and review our pasts; we need to feel fully. But in our time and culture we have lost perspective and proportion.

Some therapists are distracting us from worthwhile living in the present by concentrating on extended reviews of the tragedies of our pasts (actually such stories of tragedy are only a part of the epic of our pasts) and obsession with feelings that some "professional" has decided ought to be there.

What sorts of orientations are characteristic of CL?

Both Morita and Naikan emphasize the method and not the teacher. They direct us to develop our own potential without depending on some other person with supposedly superior powers. The instructor is merely a guide, a sounding board, an adviser. Zen teachers, too, use the metaphor of the finger pointing at the moon. "I am only the pointing finger," they say, "not the moon. Don't confuse the two."

Characteristic orientations mark the teacher/practitioner of Constructive Living. Most notable is the lack of separation between the teacher's life and the way of living he or she is teaching. CL is not an approach to helping others that is used only in the office setting. It must permeate one's own life or there is no reason or qualification to teach it to others.

The model underlying the practice of CL is educational, not medical. We prefer terms such as "student," "teacher," "guidance," "habit," "graduation," and the like to terms such as "patient," "therapist," "healing," "symptom," and "cure."

Acceptance is a key attitude modeled by the teacher/guide. Genuine acceptance naturally leads to gratitude and a desire to serve others. Constructive action is a natural part of the whole. The guide is reality-centered, reality-confident. During the teaching sessions the guide is constantly engaged in turning the student's attention toward reality.

Are there particular techniques associated with CL?

Characteristic techniques are employed in Constructive Living, but perhaps no single technique is essential to it. Any method that promotes the student's constructive learning from reality may be used. Experiential assignments such as cleaning a public park, telephoning for a job interview, writing a letter of thanks, or shopping for fresh vegetables may be used. Daily journal assignments are common, with multiple columns and behaviors recorded separately from feelings. A detailed review of recent behaviors and their results, and quizzes about the details of surroundings, all help to redirect the student's attention away from feeling-centered self-focus.

CL instructors often use the principle of yielding more or less as it is used in the martial arts. Rather than meeting the force of the student's misconceptions head-on, the instructor uses the student's own energy, deflecting it in a desired direction. For example, "You say that you are a perfectionist, but you aren't nearly perfectionistic enough. For example, you haven't noticed where the fire exits are in this room. Be more perfectionistic in your observation of your surroundings." "You complain of guilt, but what you do to cause the guilt hasn't changed. You need more guilt." Through these unexpected remarks and the subsequent changes in behavior, the student comes to view mental states as acceptable just as they are.

The teacher/guide may listen, advise, offer koans (paradoxes) for reflection, assign readings, take walks with the student, go shopping with him/her, help clean his/her room and office, attend his/her wedding ceremony. Always the teacher reflects reality back to the student and encourages the student to recognize and act on it positively.

And you don't consider CL to fit within the domain of New Age practices?

No, Constructive Living is not New Age. It is closer to Old Hat. Perhaps you know the Zen tale about a man who goes to a Zen master for guidance but won't accept the advice he receives. The master pours his guest's cup full of tea and keeps on pouring. It overflows. His point was that when a cup is already full you cannot pour more into it. Too many of the people I see these days just want a constant trickle poured into their cups to make sure it stays filled right to the brim. They don't want to empty those cups of their familiar, though obsolete, contents. Some students are what I call "couch-wise." They have tried various psychotherapies. They have some sophistication about what can and cannot be delivered in therapy. Nevertheless, they expect to sit and talk about their feelings for hour after hour. CL takes these people by surprise.

Constructive Living makes no undelivered promises. It works to help the students control what is controllable in human life: namely, their own behavior. It is a modest but effective method for dealing with human misery.

Why do you see a special need for CL's approach to living in this era?
In the Western world we went from emotional illiteracy to an obsessive concern with emotions over the period of a hundred years or so, especially as a result of Sigmund Freud's influence. This feeling focus of modern culture conceals laziness, sloppy thinking, rationalization, and self-indulgence. Maybe there was indeed a time when many people didn't recognize what they were feeling, but now there is an overemphasis on feelings as the most important element of human life. Some people seem to be attending primarily to their own feelings, in fact building their lives around them. The need these days is not to get in touch with feelings but with the reality of circumstances.

Consider how the word "feeling" has spilled over its natural boundaries into other areas of human existence. Some speakers say, "I feel (would) like a hamburger for lunch." Others say, "I feel (believe) that she did commit the crime." In Japan a major advertising campaign was centered on the phrase "I feel Coke." How lazy we have become! How undisciplined in our behavior! Constructive Living doesn't ask anyone to give up feeling. But we must beware of overindulging the feeling side of our lives. When we focus exclusively on emotions we neglect other important aspects of living. We must balance our awareness of feelings with attentive, purposeful action in the world. "Every man feels instinctively that all the beautiful sentiments in the world weigh less than a single lovely action," wrote James Russell Lowell.

Until recently we seem to have had the two alternatives of (1) individual freedom with all its concomitant social ills—teenage suicides, violence, crime, unwanted pregnancies, social unrest—or (2) social control with increasing restrictions to protect and control. Now, through Constructive Living, we are offered a third possibility: freedom in the areas that are genuinely free and self-control in the areas that require personal and social responsibility. CL doesn't make it easy to give up smoking; nor does it produce laws that make it difficult to smoke. It merely tells you that the desire to smoke is uncontrollable and that, regardless of that desire, you either smoke or you don't. Notice that there is no talk here of deciding to give up smoking or making a commitment to quit smoking or getting motivated to stop smoking. You either stop or you don't. That is reality. The rest is just smoke talk.

Before, it seemed that we had only the two alternatives of expressing feelings or suppressing them. These alternatives were couched in terms of open, honest portrayal of emotions or dishonest, unhealthy censoring of them. A third alternative that Constructive Living presents is honest recognition and acceptance of our feelings without the requirement of expressing them behaviorally.

Over the past twenty years or so reality has demonstrated that Constructive Living is not only an effective method for coping with the suffering caused by existing neuroses but that it can be used to prevent neuroses and minimize the negative effects of stress.

Queries from a student

Here is an exchange that took place with a perceptive reader of the articles about Constructive Living. Such thoughtful questions helped me to clarify my own thinking and to explain CL ideas in more detail.

How does CL differ from psychotherapy in its attitude toward the self?

CL is education, not psychotherapy. I don't know how to "fix" a mind, but I do know how to give it information and assignments. (I doubt that anyone else has a good read on how to "fix" a mind either, but that is beside the point.) There are many varieties of psychotherapy in the West. Many of them, especially the so-called psychodynamic therapies, invest a lot of time having the clients talk about themselves. In other words, clients believe that they are "working on" their problems merely by sitting and talking about themselves and their feelings. The most frequently used question in these psychodynamic therapy settings is "How do you feel about that?" It thus directs the client's attention to feelings as though they were the most important topic for discussion. As feelings are directly uncontrollable, the result is increased dependence on the therapist because the clients keep focusing on their weak point (feelings). Behavior therapies are less open to criticism on this ground, but there is still a focus on fixing feelings (after all, that is what the client appears to desire) through making cognitive and behavioral changes. In CL the feelings may change or they may not—that is not a goal of our educational process.

Why does CL promote paying less attention to the self and its satisfactions . . . isn't that the way to happiness?

Who is happy all the time? Happiness is a fine feeling, but it is well down on the list of important priorities in life. Getting done what needs to be done in life, keeping promises, doing what is right, finding satisfaction in one's lifestyle, behaving kindly and courteously, being a good steward of one's personal and shared resources, and so forth are, in my opinion, more valuable to living a good life than having a happy feeling. And we all know that no feeling (including happy ones) lasts forever.

What's wrong with selfishness? Is it just a moral issue?

Selfishness in the sense in which it is usually used is simply shortsighted and narrow. In CL thought, each person decides what he or she needs to be done. We take into consideration our feelings, desires, goals, the needs of those around us, our environment, and so forth. To consider our own feelings and desires alone isn't likely to pay off in the long run (we can define "long run" in a number of ways, but the principle still holds, I believe).

Water, Snow, Water

If self leads to focus on feelings, what's wrong with that?

Feelings contain information for us, but that information is not the only information available to us. Obsessing about feelings is too narrow a focus. We operate most satisfactorily when we fit ourselves skillfully into our circumstances. That includes working to change those circumstances.

If not self-satisfaction, then what is the basis of purpose?

Purpose and goal-direction are used interchangeably in CL. Purposes arise. I have no idea where they arise from. Perhaps they arise from the same source as thoughts or fresh moments. Sometimes my purposes are clearly related to my needs (when eating, for example). Sometimes they are more directly related to others' needs (for example, when I serve lunches at the local Senior Citizens' Center). You could argue that anything I do is self-satisfying either directly or indirectly, but that makes the term so broad as to be meaningless.

What can you do with unpleasant feelings?

Temporary helps are distraction, waiting, and using behavior and thinking to influence those feelings indirectly. The best long-term solution is merely to notice and accept them and then get on with life. The more one tries to "fix" them, the more trouble they may cause.

In dealing with others why shouldn't you look out for yourself?

A Zen answer might be that others *are* you. Another kind of answer would suggest that there is payoff for yourself in dealing compassionately with others. Another is simply that kindness and courtesy are necessary.

Where do feelings of resentment, deprivation, and the like come from?

I have no idea where any feelings come from. There are many theories about their source. If you believe one or more of the theories, that belief might be helpful or harmful to you. Choose your beliefs carefully and reexamine them now and again. We can all agree that feelings occur. What we cannot agree on is why—look at all the theories of psychology out there.

What does CL teach as a more realistic view of self/world?

A realistic view of the self/world is closer to old Chinese paintings with their tiny people depicted in huge mountain settings than to modern photos with their close-ups of human faces and tiny backgrounds. The occasional earthquake, tornado, forest fire, flood, and the like remind us of our small place in the large scheme of things. More individually speaking—aging, illness, accidents, and death remind us of the position we occupy in our circumstances.

What is CL reflection? Why is it valuable? Is gratitude a natural outcome of it?

CL reflection asks us to look at the ways in which we have been supported by people and things even when we didn't notice it or were focused on how little we were receiving. We have selectively misrepresented our past and present circumstances in order to sustain a self-image that we have overcome past obstacles and, thanks to our own efforts alone, have attained the success of our current state. The truth is that we have been takers from before we were born (taking nourishment from our mothers' bloodstream) and continue to accept the gifts of our surroundings with little notice or appreciation. The notion that we can be "burned-out" from giving so much and receiving so little is foolish. It is convenient to blame our parents, society, spouses, race, economic status, genetics, childhood experiences, God, or whatever else is in vogue at the moment for our current suffering. But someone grew and transported and bought and prepared our food; someone made our clothing and bought it or gave us the money to buy it; someone taught us our language and our strategies for solving our problems.

I don't always deserve these gifts. Sometimes I am unkind, thoughtless, stupid, grumpy. But reality (as it is embodied in people and things, energy, etc.) keeps on giving me these gifts whether I deserve them or not. Such a realization is likely to produce gratitude. But, fear not, gratitude also passes away over time unless it is restimulated. So I forget and take all this support as my due, complaining at times when I don't get exactly what I want when I want it. Then I notice again.

But won't this make you feel small and powerless?

In some ways I *am* small and powerless. To try to convince myself that I am always in complete control, that I operate only from my own resources, that I am a perfectly wonderful human being all the time is simply unrealistic. CL aims to produce a realistic view of the world, ourselves included. Then we don't need to invest so much energy in sustaining the lies that have been supporting an inflated view of self.

What are some practical exercises that can help us to overcome self-centeredness and live in a more natural way?

Many are listed in CL books—for example, *A Handbook for Constructive Living* (Honolulu: University of Hawai'i Press, 2002). Here are a few:

Perform a service for someone else. Make a list of those people thanks to whom you are able to provide that service. Even our kindness to others is a gift from others.

Similarly, list three of your finest accomplishments. Which of them did you do perfectly? Who else contributed to those accomplishments?

Interview someone who irritates you. Let them do most of the talking. Listen carefully to what they have to say about themselves.

Find out the birthday of a neighbor or someone at work or school and send that person a handmade birthday card.

Help someone do a chore that they usually do alone.

An assignment for a person with a great deal of self-focus is to limit speech to ten sentences a day but allow unlimited questions about others.

Ten words of appreciation and/or ten words of praise are acceptable as a daily assignment. Words of praise generally indicate recognition of a well-rendered service.

Write a letter of appreciation to a teacher, a trash collector, a police officer, a store manager, or a relative focusing on what you received from them this year (or the most recent year you had contact with them).

Make a list of people thanks to whom your ill family member receives medical/social care.

Write a thank-you note to someone who made it possible for you to be where you are today.

Getting Along with Life

There is something about the moment of acting that frees us from worries, fixations, and unrealistic concerns. Of course we need to plan for the future and review our pasts; we need to feel fully. But in our time and culture we have lost perspective and proportion. Some therapists are distracting us from sensible living in the present with their extended reviews of the tragedies of our pasts (actually such stories of tragedy are only a part of the epic of our pasts). Some therapists distract us from sensible living by their obsession with feelings that a supposed expert has decided ought to be there.

There are too many pseudo-wise men and women writing too many books these days. Their guru wisdom tends to merge and fade. It is too easy to read a book and then put it up on a shelf and forget the contents, knowing that other books will have other information at the next read. In the past people acquired their wisdom in small and measured portions from one or two wise old mentors at a time. There was time to digest meanings and put wisdom into practice. As the Talmud points out, "To know and not to do is not to know."

Constructive Living is meaningful realism. What foolishness masquerades as good advice! Recently I watched a program on television that purported to explain why people overeat. People told stories about unloving mothers and "eating" because of their anger, unconscious motives, and hidden feelings, and of rescues by therapists and pop-psychology books. No evidence was offered to support these offered reasons for why people overeat, but they were presented as if they were accepted truth. In fact, explaining current misbehavior by childhood traumas and unconscious motivations is mythology, much closer to religion than to science. They also become excuses for antisocial and inappropriate behavior. Sensible therapists these days offer support for constructive action. It is easier to talk about one's hidden motivations than to clean up one's behavior.

The more members of a society come to believe such absurd theories, the more social problems will appear. Why should anyone be responsible for any behavior if we are all victims of our pasts and motivated by our unconscious emotion-driven states of mind? Even crime becomes society's fault, or one's parents' fault, or the product of an unfortunately disturbed mind. Physicians, psychotherapists, social scientists, clerics, and healers are all storytellers. They construct plausible, interesting, and sometimes useful tales for their clients. To the degree that their clients find the tales to be useful explanations, predictors, and advice, they are believed and passed along to others. Less helpful tales are forgotten or misremembered and remolded into more understandable stories.

It is relatively easy to fool people with talk about getting through life with no effort. Some hypnotists claim that they can solve weight problems without their subjects dieting, exercising, or putting forth any effort. Many people will try these easy paths first precisely because they sound like they require little effort. It may take a while before they come around to a realistic though not-so-easy path, such as Constructive Living. You know what I mean. CL helps prevent us from becoming pudding people. It is exactly for people who have drifted from a realistic perspective on life that CL is most effective. Its purpose is to create a realistic, grounded, and practical individual. Constructive Living assignments prompt the student to keep bumping up against reality and to learn from these experiential encounters with ordinary life. It is just what this world needs today.

For example, today I had planned to go to the post office at 8:30 a.m. But I woke to find one of those rare days of snow in Coos Bay.

The roads will be dangerous until the snow melts: most people living on Oregon's South Coast aren't used to driving in snow. I don't have to go to the post office as planned. But if someone fell ill and needed to get to the emergency room at the local hospital I would take a shot at driving in the snow. Of course! We take into consideration the conditions (snow or high winds or anger or grief) and do what is necessary. There is nothing special about that. Nothing makes cleaning toilets fun, but they need to be cleaned. Cutting your own or your child's hair without any prior experience is scary; you may have no confidence that you can do it. But you do it if it needs to be done.

Shinks

The Japanese describe some people as *"shinkeishitsu."* The term refers to people who are tense, nervous, worried, introspective, and self-critical. In Constructive Living we call people in their moments of distress "shinks." One of the core characteristics of shinks is self-centeredness. The person who fears flying knows that the airline flies that same route day after day without crashing. But the shink believes that because he or she will be on that plane it is special, it will deviate from the usual and crash. Similarly, the shy person believes that the eyes of everyone are on him or her. It is as though everyone were watching for the shy person's slightest mistake. Of course, the reality is that we are not the center of everyone else's universe.

"Shinkiness" is filled with self-concern—what will happen to me? How terrible they make me feel! Why must I suffer so much? There is very little concern with inconveniences to others. The person suffering from a fear of flying is not particularly concerned with what might happen to the other passengers on the plane. The shink may corner anyone who shows some compassion and then complain endlessly. When the listener finally begs to be relieved of the burden of offering a shoulder to cry on, the shink will only be disappointed that the person wasn't there for him or her longer; there was so much more to say.

To some degree we all come in a shink-wrapped package. In our shinky moments we analyze our successes and failures to excess. We seek to understand our hidden motivations and subtle feelings. One young man was doing well during a workshop, so he kept asking himself whether he was putting forth so much effort in order to show off, to garner praise, or because of some genuine desire for personal development. This obsession distracted him from doing even better. In this sense, shinks are half-baked scientists. They make up hypotheses over and over again about why they do what they do, but they don't test their hypotheses against reality. They simply believe them. One false hypothesis is that shinks suffer from constant feelings of inferiority. If they truly had feelings of inferiority they would see their mistakes and failures as natural, but instead they get down on themselves for making mistakes and criticize themselves for being failures. They believe that they ought to do better than they have done in the past. Shinks try to do the impossible, then they berate themselves for failing to meet their own impossible standards. For example, feeling tension before an important business presentation or a blind date or a job interview is often natural, but shinks don't accept the naturalness. Instead they seek somehow to erase the tension they feel. Neurosis is a matter of distracted attention. The more one focuses attention on the suffering—noticing how unpleasant it is, trying to get rid of it, wishing it didn't exist, comparing the self with others who don't appear to suffer in this way, worrying about when the suffering will appear next, emphasizing other difficulties related to the suffering, complaining that the suffering is greater than is deserved and can be endured, and so forth—the more one's attention is diverted from everyday tasks and responsibilities and joys. When everyday life isn't lived well, with focused attention, a variety of new problems emerge—perhaps bills aren't paid, shopping is forgotten, deadlines are missed, accidents occur. Because suffering is often blamed for these problems, when they are noticed at all, even more attention is focused on the suffering. Gradually, attention is distanced farther and farther from everyday life. Understandably, life takes on a dreary, depressed, hopeless emotional hue.

How, then, to prevent or diminish neurosis? Humor helps give us perspective on the imaginative skills of the neurotic. Maintaining a life rhythm with exercise, proper nutrition, and enough (but not too much) sleep is also helpful. Constructive Living recommends being clear about purposes, knowing what is controllable and what is uncontrollable, and acting with consistency even when feelings fluctuate. In our neurotic moments it is important to remember that we need not, should not, try to recover from them. We must do what needs doing—not to effect a cure, but to accomplish the purpose. It is just fine to be anxious now and then.

Shigehisa Aoki considers there to be a couple of vicious spirals in neurosis. Morita had noted the upward spiral between focusing attention on a neurotic problem (a phobia, shyness, or psychosomatic area of weakness) and increased sensitivity in that area. This sensitivity draws more attention to the problem, and so on. Dr. Aoki adds another spiral. Neurotic focus leads to imperfect attention being paid to the business of everyday life. These failings lead to more misery and focus on the neurotic complaints.

I can add a few more vicious spirals to these. Neurotic self-focus leads to interpersonal problems, and these in turn increase the focus on the self (in this case, one's own limitations and inability to interact skillfully). Related spirals include a peaked interest in seeking help in order to obtain one's share of attention and expressions of concern. Such neediness and emphasis on receiving/taking from others can drive others away or force them to become more concerned with getting their share too. Thus a decrease in supply and an increase in demand are perceived all around, increasing the self-concern and self-focus of neurosis. Another related spiral is that the neurotic person's concentration on inner distress lessens his/her ability to notice and respond to cues from the external environment, including the cues offered by others. Missing important cues results in various mishaps and interpersonal failures. These real-life stressors result in more self-focus and withdrawal from external cues. And the downward spiral continues.

A woman calls out to the thief stealing her bike, "Stop! Stop!"— and, surprisingly, he does! It is clear that the woman knows the social rule against stealing bikes, whereas the thief does not know that he doesn't have to stop when his victim demands he do so. Later on, that same woman is being caressed by her boyfriend. She says "Stop! Stop!"—and he stops. It is clear that both of them share the same rules for lovemaking. There are social rules for being neurotic as well. One is expected to be self-focused and admit to suffering. One is expected to try to overcome one's problems and seek help in solving them. One is expected to have low self-esteem, to complain, to show impaired judgment, to lead a severely limited life, to hope for some miraculous cure, and to believe that no one suffers as one does. More specifically, shinks believe: (1) I suffer alone (no one else suffers like I do, so no one else can truly understand my misery); (2) all I do is suffer (I experience only suffering, there is no support or positive experience in my life). Furthermore, shinks are sure that they are almost always right or almost always wrong (about suffering and anything else).

Shinks

4

Common Sense

It's not common sense! It doesn't even fit your own experience! Nevertheless, some people have swallowed the pill-sized doses of mental health beliefs excusing all sorts of hurtful behaviors because of strong feelings or poor experiences in childhood. You've been told that teachers and parents can instill self-esteem and self-confidence in a child, that children (or adults, for that matter) need self-esteem before they can accomplish anything. There are two kinds of foolishness here. First, you don't need self-esteem or self-confidence to get done what you need to do in life. When you start out on any new undertaking you are unlikely to begin it with the assurance that you will succeed. You do your best and sometimes you do succeed. When people tell you that you have done a good job, when you see the desired results of your work, it is then that you begin to feel confidence in your ability to do the job well, not before you begin it. So you can begin a project without self-confidence; just begin.

The second fallacy is that someone else can give you self-confidence or self-esteem. You don't receive self-confidence, you earn it. You know that from your own experience. Self-esteem is earned through effort and success. It cannot be conferred on someone by a teacher or a parent or a therapist or anyone else. We acquire self-confidence after we have tried doing something and have succeeded at it, not before. Thinking won't produce self-confidence. Neither will talking to someone. You have to put your ideas into the arena of action, risking failure, in order to earn self-confidence. No one can talk you into it.

Those of you who have been alive long enough to experience your first days on a new job, do you remember how you hoped you wouldn't make too many mistakes, how you dreaded appearing foolish and inept? You didn't start your new job brimming with confidence. But after a while, when people began to praise you for doing your work well, the self-confidence began to emerge. Perhaps you had a similar experience when starting out at a new school in your youth. Freshmen rarely have the confidence about getting around to classes that juniors and seniors have earned through experience. As C. S. Lewis wrote, "What I like about experience is that it is such an honest thing . . . you may have deceived yourself, but experience is not trying to deceive you. The universe rings true whenever you fairly test it."

I suppose what people mean by self-esteem is feeling good about yourself and feeling confident. But those feelings are elusive and temporary. It is better to build a history of living life fully, and the way to build that history is to live life fully now. You can't change the past; you can't live in the future; all you have to work with is now. Then, from the point of view of next week and next year, this now becomes the past; this now becomes your history. You change yourself by changing what you do now. One of the problems with making the achievement of more self-confidence one's primary, immediate goal is that it focuses attention on introspection (Do I have enough self-esteem yet?) and distracts us from the forward/outward orientation that gets things done in life. Accomplishing goals in life often creates self-confidence as a side effect.

In order to sustain some measure of self-esteem without the effort of activity and risk we have come up with socially accepted excuses. It is easier to say that you are depressed than to admit that you are lazy. Additional excuses for not making an effort include:

My history, my upbringing, my genes;
My illness, my handicap, my neurotic quirks;

My education, my IQ, my race, my culture;
My business partner, my spouse, my parents;
My boss, my supervisor, my manager, my coworkers;
The economy, the times, the society, the government;
My enemy, my rival, my ex-spouse, the devil.

Trying to support a constant image of self-esteem makes you purposely seek to ignore your real weak moments, your real unkind moments, your past failures. It is better to focus on how supportive other people and things have been to you, and how to offer them some repayment. When the focus is on the self one generally feels miserable; one concentrates on getting one's own share from the world. A giving attitude toward behavior is more satisfying. But, don't worry, gratitude will fade over time, too, just like any other feeling (sadness, happiness, embarrassment, any feeling passes with time, doesn't it?). It is best just to be realistic, recognizing the whole mix of good and bad, confident and unconfident, wise and foolish, receiving and returning.

You probably know people from disrupted families who have turned out to be positive, contributing members of society. It is seductively convenient to blame our own inadequacies on our parents. It is easy to sit and talk about the supposed causes of our limitations rather than getting out and working on changing them. What you are invited to ignore and forget in some forms of Western psychotherapy is the reality that the people who raised you, however imperfect they may have been, also fed and clothed you, taught you language and life, perhaps are still contributing to your economic and psychological support. You know that you must shoulder responsibility for your own actions despite the excuses provided by pseudo-experts in the psychology, social work, and the legal systems. Society never makes us do what we do. Race never makes us do what we do. Our upbringing never makes us do what we do. *We* do what we do. "In the end, we are all the sum total of our actions . . . we write our own destiny; for inexorably we become what we do. This, I believe, is the supreme logic and law of life" (Madame Chiang Kai-shek).

Water, Snow, Water

Research psychologists measure self-esteem with pencil-and-paper tests. They assume that our measure of ourselves can be recorded with little marks on paper. They speak about self-esteem as a constant—that is, relatively unchanging over time—because they either take one snapshot of it with their tests or a few snapshots over a period of time using the same tests in the same test environments. How foolish! Does anyone think that our evaluations of ourselves remain unchanged immediately after we have made an embarrassing blunder or after we have completed a difficult task successfully? Of course the way we feel about ourselves changes from moment to moment. I have never experienced a moment of "average-level" self-esteem. Research psychologists had better begin to understand how our minds work by examining their own. I'm willing to bet they feel better about themselves when they receive news of their promotion to full professorship and esteem themselves less when they see themselves as the cause of a beloved someone leaving them. Although introspection is out of fashion in research psychology and counting/manipulating numbers is in, researchers need not waste time on useless measuring devices. Of course, they can define "self-esteem" any way they like. However, to define it as unchanging over time or existing as some sort of statistical-mean level is to make the term relatively useless in everyday life. Unrealistic variables may produce correlations and nice tables for research conference slides and computer presentations. They just don't mean much for us here on the ground.

Some people would have you develop self-pride through participation in the men's movement or the women's movement. I'm not sure where that pride is supposed to come from. Take the men's movement for example. We males became males thanks to the Y chromosome of our fathers, requiring no effort on our part. We grew to become men thanks to the food raised by both males and females—grocers, delivery people, employers, and so on. Should we take pride in our resulting actions? Those actions were fueled by the food we were given. The values we have were taught to us directly or indirectly by others, male and female. We learned much of our manhood verbally, using words taught to us by both sexes. About the only thing I can find that is a basis for male pride is my pride itself—and that seems to be based on an egocentric and systematic refusal to notice the contributions of others to anything I can call mine. Why waste time trying to create a cotton-candy self-pride, male or female? Isn't it more realistic to face life with humility, recognizing how small the footprint of humanity is on the large field of nature? Forest fires, volcanoes, earthquakes, tornados, and glaciers remind us of our proper place in the scheme of things.

5

Fleeing from Responsibility for Behavior

A young man kills his abusive stepfather and then expects to be excused for his action. The United States wages war in another country for what it considers righteous reasons and expects the victims of war to love and support us. A young person tells the truth about a delinquent acquaintance and is surprised by the repercussions. It is certainly proper to do what is right. But too many people these days appear to believe that if they do what they believe to be right they should pay no price for their actions. Compare this attitude to the actions of the Japanese samurai who avenged their master's death and then killed themselves, or the terrorists who gave their lives for their cause, however misguided. We must do what is right (having courage or not) and accept the personal consequences. Upholding one's principles is worth personal sacrifice.

You might think, perhaps, that unconscious feelings are the cause of hurtful actions. You may have been taught that you have hidden feelings in your psyche of which you are not aware, that you can go to mental health professionals who somehow discern what these hidden feelings are, that you can express these feelings, get them out in the open, and they will no longer bother you. Hundreds of years ago people were taught that they had evil spirits in their hearts, that they could go to religious professionals who would somehow discern what those evil spirits were and help expel them through exorcism. There is no essential difference between these two services except that the one suggesting that you get in touch with your hidden feelings is more popular these days. If expressing a feeling gets rid of it, then telling someone "I love you" should lead to indifference.

It is not that we have a more sophisticated understanding of the human mind than people in the past did. It is merely that we have different myths about the mind. Trying to make sense of how we think and feel and what we do is and has been important to all humans in all cultures and times. Any set of myths about the mind has some usefulness and some blind spots. Recent experimental research does show that some processes of the brain occur outside of our awareness, but not in the simple sense promoted by Freudians in the last century. Beware of the myths created by oversimplifications of some MRI and fMRI studies. We are still a long way from revealing specific thoughts through brain scans.

An Oregon businessman wrote me this in a letter: "I have been going through a confusing period. Because of current economic conditions I recently closed a business that I spent many years building from nothing. My family and friends are constantly talking about how depressed I am and that I am in mourning for the loss. But I am not. Closing the business is not a good thing, it is not a bad thing, it just is. However, I have been told how I am so much that I was beginning to believe that I should be or that I had these feelings and didn't know it! So hearing you this morning was like a breath of fresh air. Thank you."

There is no question that some readers, without ever having met this man, would consider him "in denial." "In denial" is a relatively new phrase—denial has become something like a room one enters. There is little or no evidence this businessman could conceivably provide that would convince such readers that he is not hiding deep sorrow within walls of suppression. Beware of such prejudicial evaluations. They are based on no more than modern myths of the mind.

"Are you happy?" "Do you like yourself?" "Are you satisfied with your life?" If you can offer a quick, global yes or no answer to these questions then you aren't thinking clearly. Perhaps you have been influenced by pop psychology to come up with acceptable answers to simple-minded questions. My guess is that sometimes you are happy, sometimes not. Sometimes you like yourself, sometimes not. Sometimes you are satisfied with your life, sometimes not. More useful questions involve exploration of the conditions under which you are sometimes happy, sometimes not, sometimes liking yourself, sometimes not, sometimes satisfied, sometimes not. Moreover, I suspect that there are many moments of our lives in which these questions are irrelevant, when they cannot be answered meaningfully at all. For example, when you are fully involved in some engrossing task you are neither happy nor unhappy, just absorbed. But if you watch daytime talk shows you'll see that oversimplified questions and no-brain answers are as common as commercials.

So what can be done about this detour from common sense, this diversion from reality to fatuous fantasy? First, think about how you talk about your thoughts, feelings, and behavior. Talk in ways that really fit your experience, not using the vocabulary you have picked up from television and magazines. Second, doubt the so-called experts on your mind. There aren't any, including the author of this book. *You* are the expert on the workings of your own mind. You alone have lived with it. When you aren't feeling something why should you believe someone who tells you the opposite? Third, consider the real payoff in buying into current myths of the mind. It may be convenient to blame your parents or society or your race or economic status for your current suffering, but such thinking leaves you a passive victim with no possible way out, except, perhaps, the airy dream game of expensive psychotherapy. There is a better chance of turning your life around by getting done what you need to do in your life, constructively. Don't wait to feel motivated or confident or empowered. Don't wait for some mind fix. Just get on with your life. Do what needs doing. Once more, when you tire of mere insightful talk come to Constructive Living. Join us in the doing of life. CL is where the action is.

Let's be clear that I don't feel resentment toward all psychotherapists. I'm not into generalized therapy bashing. Most of my working/

research/informal time has been spent with these professionals. But I really do believe that some therapists practicing some forms of insight-oriented traditional Western therapy actually do harm while believing they are doing high-class work. I want to shock them a bit, and so I may alienate some of the good guys. I'm sorry that I'm not sufficiently skillful at writing to accomplish that first purpose while avoiding the alienation. As there are only a few more than three hundred certified CL instructors around the world our approach to mental health poses no obvious threat to entrenched providers of psychotherapy. Rather, we offer some tools that may not have been previously considered. I was surprised to find on the Internet a while back that the Maine Psychological Association listed Morita therapy as one of the acceptable therapies for billing right up there with psychoanalysis, behavior therapy, and others. If you are looking for a psychotherapist, I suggest you turn your attention to one who has a more modern, behavioral orientation.

One reason I write as I do is because of the feedback of those who kindly take the time to contact me about the influence of CL ideas they put into practice in their daily lives after being misled by insight-only, feeling-focused therapists. They have been led to accept what I consider unbelievable stories about why they are as they are and then left with no suggestions or advice about how or what to change (what to do next). Psychotherapists, too, kindly write to me about the usefulness of CL principles in their practice. Here are some typical examples from readers of a variety of CL books and articles and media interviews:

"I have begun to experience some of the benefits of a 'Just Do It' approach to life. . . . As a therapist who has long worked with the delinquent population, I have seen firsthand the destruction of spirit that can result from people waiting until they feel good enough to undertake a particular task. Your writing so concisely describes what I have long believed, that we can create tomorrow's past with today's actions." (ML, Iowa)

"Yesterday, I went over to Border's Books (across the street from my workplace downtown) during a break, seeking yet another of those fluffy New Age Creative Thought manifestation handbooks. My original intention was to research a different kind of magical thinking in order to deal with some life situations that are not what I'd like them to be.

"Your books were shelved not far from the 'think strongly and it shall be given unto you' author's output. For some reason, my eyes and hands strayed. I wound up at the cash counter with two books, one of them a copy of your *Handbook for Constructive Living*. I took it home last night. I read it twice. I took notes. I slapped my thighs. I laughed out loud. I winced. I said, Aha! Finally, I closed the book for the second time at 2 a.m. with a big Bravo! and 'Where do I find out more about this Constructive Living stuff?' . . . Thank you, again, for your work. I've already found your words helpful, inspiring and above all, PRACTICAL. Today I used CL to help me with my most chronic, irritating problem area: getting to work in the mornings (I really dislike the job), and I now have concrete proof of CL's efficacy with a real-world situation. I want more! CL is certainly worth serious, sustained effort." (LP, Washington)

"I have done some of the exercises and found them enormously helpful, as well as painful and poignant. I now do simple Naikan reflection often throughout the day, when sitting in traffic or waiting in line or holding on the phone. I find it especially helpful to do it whenever I feel oppressed, or feel that other people are demanding too much of my time, my space or whatever. I stop, reflect on my mother, father, and other people and things that have supported me, and I realize I can never do enough to repay what I have received.

"I was interested in the essays on work because I've always had attitude problems about my job, and lately my work had been lax and careless. I was caught in a quandary of wondering if I should change jobs, if that would really help, what did I want to do, etc. Through reading and listening to CL material I have realized a few things:

"I can stop judging my work on the basis of whether or not it has some intrinsic worth or merit; I needed to establish a purpose for myself and see if that purpose could be accomplished via this job. I have identified my purpose, and it can be accomplished here. The game of whether your job is worthwhile or not is a losing one; even doctors who save lives must know that eventually their patients will die, even if only of old age. Architects see their buildings torn down. No matter what you do, it won't last forever and it won't always be so very important, permanent or perfect.

"I can do every action with attention, and realize the value of the tools I use and how I am supported by them.

"I can be aware of how my every action is an opportunity to treat people well, use resources wisely, use tools properly and with attention, and repay my debt to the university. It is not a law of the universe that a job must be interesting, fun or exciting. I am not a loser or a failure if my job is not interesting, fun or exciting. These insights and many others were really helpful, and now I am able to do my job more efficiently and with less mental strain and despair." (AM, New Jersey)

"My husband is currently suffering from depression. He complains a lot about his work, his pain, his worthlessness. He often yells at our daughter. I do daily Naikan and therefore have a record of gifts and troubles. One night when feeling especially sad and frustrated with my husband's behaviors (complaining) I retrieved a month's worth of journal entries. From these entries I wrote my husband a thank you note for doing 32 laundries, washing the dishes 71 times, vacuuming and mopping the floors 4 times, leaving work early to pick our daughter up from soccer practice 6 times and attending all of her soccer games, regardless of how badly she behaves. I described, in great detail, four delicious meals he prepared and two family dinners he took the family out to eat, the time he changed the oil in my car. I added detail on why I valued these gifts and recognized that many are given regardless of the trouble our daughter and I cause, regardless of his pain, regardless of his lack of energy. I left the note in the seat of his car and went to work.

"That night I arrived home to find a bouquet of two dozen roses and a smile and hug from my husband. He said, 'I never knew you counted the laundries.' I wrote the note to ease a debt. I accrued more debt. My husband enjoyed feelings of being appreciated. He saw his worth to the family. The relationship goes on. CL is reflection and action. I cannot control my husband's behavior or feelings. I can reflect; I can act. P.S. We have been married for 29 difficult and joy-filled years." (AN, Vermont)

"I've developed a philosophy very close to CL while working with overweight clients at a major weight loss chain. Most of them have been to all kinds of therapy and O.A. to explore the cause of their eating disorders—with little success. I work to bring them into the present—accepting what is—and then taking action to change it." (BW, Indiana)

"I wrote you a few days ago to express interest in Constructive Living. I just wanted to tell you my experience this morning. I am coming back from a two-year back problem that I allowed to run my life. I am now getting better all the time. Anyway, I felt extremely wrung out and felt like just laying [*sic*] down. My apartment is very unorganized and dusty; out of hand! It seemed like an overwhelming task, but I needed to get started on it, one reason being that my asthma gets so bad if I do not have simple clean surroundings. Also if I live in clutter my mind seems to follow suit. I remembered from one of your writings that you can still do what you need to do, even if you don't feel like doing it! So, I set a timer for ten minutes (because I thought I could do at least ten minutes!) and I just slowly worked mindfully and slowly and did an excellent job. Once I started I was able to work for one whole hour. I was pleased as punch! I can't say that I feel wonderful or untired, but I have a sense of satisfaction. It seems to be a simple idea to just do it, even if you do not particularly FEEL like it.

Fleeing from Responsibility for Behavior

I believe it was William James who said that he did two things every day that he did not feel like doing. I forgot why he did that. I just wanted to let you know that for one woman, me, you have made a profound difference in my life. Thank you for writing and compiling the books." (JJ, Internet)

"I really like practicing Naikan, though it's not always a pleasant experience. I had always resisted the religious notion of serving God and society. In fact, my internal concept of God had become one of a kind of super prison warden keeping all us earthly inmates in line with the threat of hell. . . . By substituting the concept Reality for the concept God, I understand that I do have real debts, many more than I can ever hope to repay. Reality has been very generous to me, starting with my parents and extending to the efforts of many people that I will never meet. Literally 'counting my blessings' is making a really big difference in how I act in this world. Thanks for telling me about that." (TL, Kentucky)

"I can hardly describe the weight I felt lifting from my shoulders as I read the CL interview. The break-up of my marriage over the last few months has been the catalyst of some real soul searching and spiritual growth. . . . The cynic in me wondered if all I was doing was contributing to this self-help juggernaut industry by ordering the tapes, books and videos. Then I read your interview. It made so much sense. Someone out there is saying it's okay to feel guilty and it's healthy! The Naikan concept of reality confidence and reality esteem says accept your full range of uncontrollable emotions and forget about 'ruminating' about all this. Control what you can do and get to work repaying the world for all you take, don't blame it for what you perceive you have not been given." (HL, Vermont)

"I have many acquaintances and a few friends who seem almost obsessed by the real or perceived trauma[s] that they suffered some time in their past. I, too, at least for a while, tried to rationalize my own 'failure' by finding fault with something my parents must have done or didn't do during my youth. . . . I now look back on my own imperfections and my parents' forgiveness of me and am filled with much gratitude. Having raised two children to adult and near adulthood I am filled with remorse that I ever thought of blaming my parents for my being the imperfect person that I am." (RH, Indiana)

"I am relatively new to this path and stumble often, sometimes even crashing. I have put off this letter several times, feeling as though I had no right to pursue this until I was much better at living constructively. Much of my life has been not-acting according to feeling instead of acting according to purpose. Oh well, there is only this letter being written now. . . . Several years ago when I was in college a professor introduced me to a few Zen concepts. I found them intriguing and intellectually stimulating but was not able to apply them to my life with any great success. Since reading your works, I have reread the Zen material with new understanding and, even better, with more successful application. I am at home in Zen. How do I thank you for guiding me home again?" (TD, Wisconsin)

"I have been in conventional therapy for several months now and have made a big improvement but I am tired of digging down into all the pain of childhood and the rest of my misguided life. I want to get on with it and I need a little positive wisdom to guide me along. The Constructive Living way sounds a little like the way I was brought up but without the negative cruelty that went along with it." (GH, Arizona)

"Some of what you say I've heard many times before. How you said it made an impact. The last few weeks have included saying goodbye to a lot of my early dreams that are not reflected in my present reality. These weeks have also included doing something on a daily basis to enhance further meaning in my life." (PW, Nevada)

Fleeing from Responsibility for Behavior

"My family is going through a very bad time right now because of some bad counseling involving hypnosis to discover 'hidden' traumas. I think your advice might be helpful to those of us who would read it." (ED, Oregon)

"My husband and I have spent three years going to two different therapists for marriage counseling. Not one minute was used to teach us how to live together in the day-to-day present. They spent the whole time going through our childhoods. One used what he called 'Explosive Therapy' and the other said she was helping us to 'heal our inner child.' At the end of all this my husband and I still feel we're back on the first rung of the ladder. . . . So when I read the article about CL I was glad to find there's help without wasting time 'healing childhood.'" (CC, California)

"I've been neurotic for the last 15 of my 38 years. The result of this has been frequent battles with panic attacks. At one point several years ago I was nearly a full-blown agoraphobic. While I've worked through these problems largely on my own, I have sometimes sought the advice of experts in a vain attempt to rid myself of the severely unpleasant feelings associated with anxiety. What an insight it was to learn that there was no need to avoid these feelings; that I could instead put that effort into strengthening myself to 'take the hit' of an anxiety attack and, when it ended, move on from there. Of course, as I'm sure you're aware, once I stopped trying to avoid the attacks and turned around to face them and stand my ground, the attacks lost much of their force. Thank you for helping me to help myself calm down and reclaim part of my life." (MD, Oregon)

"I earned my Masters in Marriage and Family Therapy in May. I have been in therapy. I really feel the general therapeutic focus on what is wrong has been overemphasized and contributes to a sense of hopelessness for many clients (and therapists!). I know I personally can make a lot more movement when I look toward what is going right in my life and take action to get more of the same going. Reality is so much more important than focusing on the perceived past." (TS, California)

"I applied CL during my post-surgery days unknowingly, but evidently in my subconscious from reading your article. Needless to say I had explored and have experienced every possible emotion from tears to what I call human suffering. But I was aware of them and I just let them happen. I know there is no point trying to control what you cannot control. But my attitude throughout was let's get on with it. Get the surgery done. Let's do what needs to be done. That concept came from that CL article—I know it did." (KB, Ohio)

"I am writing to you primarily to offer my gratitude. That was not the original first sentence of this letter. As a matter of fact I had nearly completed half when I realized that as I wrote I was continually scanning the outline I had carefully prepared. Suddenly I realized that I had structured my scribbling so as to show you how much I have learned. Careful not to focus too much on feelings. Perhaps it was an attempt to convince you I already knew and had in place the concepts of Constructive Living. I don't know . . . what a good boy am I . . . what a rare specimen . . . so in line with your teachings I shouldn't even need your guidance. Well, that wouldn't have been a very honest first correspondence, but very much in line with my character. So I've started over. Pheww! It felt good to get that out. Now, where was I? . . . There is one thing that has changed dramatically: I no longer blame [my work] for my failings and shortfalls. It was so easy. I couldn't attend my children's events, social occasions, responsibilities around the house, and much more . . . I was (and still am) in a state of perpetual jetlag. I am either running like a madman to catch up with my real life or attempting to fall back in order to get rested to go [to work]. Now, however, I simply try to do what needs doing, now. I don't always triumph, but I am taking responsibility. It feels as though quite a large burden has been lifted. I am on a healthier regimen (including a daily walk), have lost

Fleeing from Responsibility for Behavior

nearly 25 pounds, and I feel great. I am keeping a journal (an organizer actually) that [sic] I record bits and pieces of my days and significant thoughts. I provide myself with quiet time daily. . . ." (LT, Washington)

"I am using CL in my daily life and also with my clients; it's gotten into my brain in a solid and useful way. One of my clients is a court reporter who has been trying to pass the exam to be certified for 6 years. Every 6 months she retakes the exam, every 6 months she does not pass. She has been working with a psychologist to 'get rid of' her nervousness so she could pass and came to me for hypnosis to really get rid of it. I had her work on noticing, had her do the exercises and give up attempts to push the nervousness away. During the exam she noticed what the examiner was saying instead of the nervousness. She has passed 2 of the 3 parts of the Kansas exam and will retake the 3rd in 6 months; she will take the Missouri exam in April. She said, 'I feel so different now, since I know I don't have to get rid of nervousness.' Thank you. It is so much easier also to say, I don't know why, and then move on to what needs to be done now." (LR, Internet)

"When I recently finished your latest book my feelings of gratitude reminded me of my own advice to my friend. I know we can't win the race to balance what we give with what we have received in this lifetime. A simple 'thank you' isn't enough, but it is what needs to be done. Thank you for writing and making CL books available at a cost well below their true value." (HG, Massachusetts)

"I've felt so angry, depressed, and cheated by life for so long, but really I have so much. I could really benefit from being less self-absorbed. I've been in therapy for eleven years with eight different therapists. I need to try something else. I'm 31 and life is just too short." (JS, Wisconsin)

"I am one of those people abused as a child, confused as an adult; and I've spent my lifetime searching for the answers. I find myself constantly trying to analyze my thoughts, my emotions, and my life. I just want to live well, healthy. I want my life to be constructive. . . . I am an extreme perfectionist; so much that I often let myself down by not living up to the expectations of one hundred people around me. Not only do I want to be perfect in my own eyes, but to everyone else as well. This Constructive Living makes so much sense. I know in my heart that one must take action to change things. I must admit I think it may be difficult at first. I mean difficult by having to change my already deep-rooted behavior of analyzing feelings and exhausting myself trying to change them." (MH, Virginia)

"I have tried traditional therapy and wasted my time and money. Thanks for your enlightened way." (PD, New York)

"I feel I've been running around in a fuzzy haze for the past two years enjoying myself but nonetheless not really directing myself or knowing my purpose. It took [the article about Constructive Living] to make me slow down, appreciate what has and is being done for me. It has made me want to show gratitude to everything [sic] concerned, especially my parents." (KS, United Kingdom)

"I was in therapy (Jungian basically) for seven years but while it was very interesting in an intellectual sense it proved to be just about useless for any real change. After giving up in disgust I adopted my grandmother's philosophy of 'Pull up your socks and get on with it,' which is the closest previous exposure I have had to anything like Constructive Living—you might be surprised how similar. Anyway, this seems like a formalized and structured approach to Gran's advice, and I know what it's done for me. So I would like to be able to pass it on to others who are fed up with navel-gazing as a way of life." (MZ, Canada)

"The CL lifeway really clicked for me this past weekend. I finally cleared up a project that had been hanging loose for weeks. In the past, I'd have congratulated myself with a cookie or brought myself a treat. But instead, my first thoughts were, 'Good, that's done. What needs doing now?' And I then completed another task that had been hanging loose for years (it was cataloging old photo negatives and pictures). Both projects went much more quickly than I expected as I lost myself in doing them. I felt pride and accomplishment when they were completed. Then, with some time on my hands after cleaning up, I thought, 'What needs to be done now?' And so I went on my power walk around the neighborhood. . . . It was a most unusual, most productive weekend. The weird thing was it was almost as if 'I' wasn't there. I experienced what you've said about one being reality's agent. A most peculiar feeling, but I can't argue with the results." (MB, Internet)

"I have been practicing CL now for about six months and have passed through the honeymoon period. I have experienced failure as well as success but I accepted it and asked myself 'What do I need to do next?' I have become good at doing what needs to be done and have experiential knowledge of the maxim 'It doesn't get easier, only different.' Your idea that paranoia is a simplification filter makes perfect sense to me. I have been on medication for paranoia since 1977 and none of the therapist's ideas have been as helpful as that one. I think that Naikan practice is going to help me not look at others so one-sidedly. Feelings are for feeling; Thoughts are for thinking; Life is for living." (BS, New York)

"I have just finished reading *Playing Ball on Running Water*. The ideas I found there speak very strongly to my frustration with years of trying Western psychotherapy and even drug therapy to try to overcome years of acute depression. On drug therapy I found that my acutely painful feelings disappeared. But, in addition to suffering finally un-bearable side effects, I was no better at living an effective and meaningful life!" (DB, Internet)

Water, Snow, Water

6

An Alternative to Psychotherapy

In the West psychotherapy is still sometimes practiced as though mental health experts exist who know more about their patients' minds than the patients do themselves. Their patients may be encouraged to talk about themselves, their current difficulties, unsatisfying emotions, disturbed relationships, and disadvantaged histories. Once the causes of the difficulties are explored and feelings "vented," the patient may be encouraged to make some changes in behavior. Psychological jargon like "addictive personality," "narcissistic personality," "empowered," "motivational deficit," and the like are employed. Such a course may actually be helpful to some patients, because any system that offers hope of gaining control over one's life is preferable to a sense of helplessness and hopelessness. There will always be a need for medicines to treat mental illness. But the neurotic suffering of healthy people is not illness; it is a sort of ignorance.

There are no truly dynamic psychotherapies in the West. Western psychotherapies are all static. They all operate, as did outmoded anthropological functionalism, with static views of the self. People prefer simple answers to their problems. "I'm neurotic! I'm a shink! That explains it!" All psychological troubles are thought to be understandable within this single, one-dimensional model. But the psyche should be understood in the context of ever-changing situations, not as a fixed construct. The problem is that we are all dynamically changing—like the weather. It does little good to produce a detailed weather map of the average weather over the course of a year—the direction of the wind, the morning and evening average highs and lows. That is what a description of personality or character is. That is what a psychiatric diagnosis is. We would find it more useful to know about the weather at a given time, perhaps today, or right now. Similarly, at any given moment we may be operating out of shinkiness or we may not. Too many clients have bought the whole "shink-wrapped" package.

Mrs. G. takes naps at home during the day. She wants to overcome her napping, which she considers a neurotic habit. She considers that habit a symptom. On the evening I learned of her napping "problem," I asked her if she had taken a nap that day during her intensive training. She had not. So I told her she was cured. "But only for today," she replied. Of course. That's the only cure possible. We humans want guarantees that not only today is secure but all the tomorrows as well. A few months later I called Mrs. G. at random to inquire whether she had taken a nap that day. On that day, too, she was cured of her napping habit.

Mrs. K. suffered from difficulty getting herself up in the morning, but she got up at 5:30 a.m. and 6:00 a.m. in order to prepare for intensive CL training. And she got up promptly every day during the training. She's cured too. Perhaps not forever. But for today. "Firewood never becomes ashes" is a Zen koan. Now firewood, now ashes.

The dangers of insight therapies are not so different from those of behavioral or pharmacological therapies. One learns to look for the "real" sources of undesired feelings, attitudes, and impulses (in the brain, the unconscious, or elsewhere). The more one feels successful in finding the "real" reasons for the problem, the more one is inclined to search in that area again the next time a problem appears. Such searching can distract one from taking action that fits the situation. One becomes dependent on searching and fixing, either by oneself or with the help of a therapist. The difference in the CL approach is that one notices the distressing feelings or whatever and gets on with life—no dependency on drugs or a therapist or insight, no need to "overcome" the problem in order to resume living.

Be careful of the notion that if we understand anxiety (even in a Constructive Living way) that we can use it or redirect it or eradicate it. My sense of the meaning of "understanding anxiety" is "accepting its existence as part of reality," not "fathoming its origins" or "analyzing its components." Medicine is necessary for mental illness, but too many feeling-focused behaviors are mislabeled as illnesses. Formulized treatment may work with many illnesses of the body, but individualization is necessary for working with neurotic disorders. Too many mental health practitioners try to use whatever formula method they learned in school with all their clients.

In describing the contribution of D. T. Suzuki, the main figure in the introduction of Zen Buddhism to the West, Shimonura (1986) makes a couple of points that are relevant to the introduction of Japanese psychotherapies to the West in general. First, he holds that where there are fundamental differences in approach any attempt to restructure the system in Western terms will inevitably result in distortion and misunderstanding. I believe that his points apply equally well to the understanding of CL's Morita therapy and Naikan as it does to Zen Buddhism. Attempts to fit Morita therapy and Naikan into a Western psychotherapy framework are unlikely to be successful, because there are fundamental differences between Eastern and Western systems of therapy. True, both Morita and Western behavioral psychotherapies challenge clients' thoughts and beliefs in a rational way, using advice, assignments, and experience. But Western psychotherapies attempt to use those changes to affect feelings directly. Adjusting feelings is, after all, what their clients seem to desire. CL, on the other hand, holds that there is something more desirable than simply relieving temporary neurotic suffering. Unlike Western psychotherapies, the Morita therapy element in CL is not about reducing anxiety or phobias; it is about living fully with them as part of one's momentary existence. The Western idea that anxiety, shyness, fears, lack of confidence, and other feeling states are accretions auxiliary to one's momentary awareness makes no sense to the true Moritist. When I am afraid, that fear IS me in that moment; it is not something extraneous that can be lopped off with clever words or chemicals. When that feeling goes away (for whatever reason), I am not the same me less only that feeling; the whole gestalt of who I am changes. What I tried to do about the feeling continues to affect me after the feeling has passed.

Shimomura makes the second point that Suzuki's insistence and examples showing that Zen thought is different helped to clarify some of the restrictions and limitations of Western philosophy. As long as we keep trying to explain Eastern therapies in Western terms we miss the lessons they hold for us. We also miss recognition of our own narrow vision and narrow approaches to overcoming neurotic habits. I specifically avoided using the phrase "narrow approaches to cure" in the previous sentence because the term "cure," too, represents the confined medical model within which much of Western therapy is practiced. Neurotic thoughts, feelings, and behaviors are not merely symptoms of some "illness" called "neurosis." They *are* the person who suffers. So they cannot be dealt with as though they were isolated symptoms of illness, like paralysis or muscle spasms. Life meaning isn't discovered through medication—unless life meaning is to be found in the faulty excuses provided by the medical establishment.

From the Moritist perspective, fears are more like fevers in that they have a useful function as well as causing discomfort. People have died of fevers, so some extreme cases may require medication, but even then no attempt is made to make a person fever-free for life. We need the capacity for fevers and fears to continue for our protection, our defense.

Similarly, the reflection element of Constructive Living, Naikan, points up the limitations of the self-esteem focus of Western approaches to mental health. Telling clients that they are wonderful and capable of doing anything they set their minds to is an easy sell in the West, however unrealistic. Advising clients to serve others as a way of working off their debts, as CL's Naikan proposes, is a harder one in the Western cultural milieu, however effective and realistic that advice may be. One is not a better human being for deeply understanding or sternly evaluating oneself. Better human beings are created through actions. It is far easier to sit in therapy and reflect on one's problems than to clean up the town's garbage or apologize to those we have wronged. Know this clearly: for all the insight you may obtain, you are what you do. Meanwhile, accept the self that criticizes and wants more, is dissatisfied and resists acceptance. Giving up and accepting the whole self is part of both the action and the reflection aspects of CL. It offers an educational alternative to psychotherapy that is practical, effective, and difficult. There are a number of books (Reynolds, 1984a, 1984b, 1986, 1987, 1989a, 1989b, 1990) describing the practice of Constructive Living and offering exercises for experiential validation of the methods.

7

Psychotherapy as Myth

Psychoanalysis, now supplanted by behavioral and chemical therapies, seems to me closer to religion than to science. Any stimuli—from dreams, writing errors, choice of clothing, word associations, diet, choice of lovers or friends or enemies or whatever—can be interpreted by someone with a reasonable imagination and some training to yield insights into the client's conflicts and problems. These insights are not gained because the stimuli are messages from the unconscious but because humans face a limited set of conflicts and problems. Any stimulus can be seen to reflect one or another of these common human difficulties. No one interprets a dream as representing anger at one's bed or attachment to one's lamp.

Some psychotherapists and psychologists think that people derive their self-image from only one part of reality—such as sexual development during childhood—the part in which they specialize and thus focus on. They are simply overspecialized and wrong. Much, much more of our experience in infancy, childhood, youth, and adulthood contributes to the development of a self-image. People like to hear simple stories explaining who they are. This writing is also one of those stories. It is up to you to decide which stories are oversimplified and untrue.

"The science game, the healing game, the knowledge game are magnificent human structures. They are our proudest game accomplishments. But they are great only so long as they are seen as games. When they go beyond this point, the trouble begins—claims to a non-game reality status: the emergence of experts, professionals, priests, status-favored authorities, claims to power and control and priority. Look at the A.E.C. Look at the A.M.A. And watch out! At this point you will find that games which began with the goal of decreasing human helplessness end up increasing it," observed Dr. Timothy Leary. The same can be said for psychotherapy—it was initiated in order to reduce human helplessness and now too often works to increase it.

One mistake psychotherapy has made is keeping people in therapy long enough to see changes in their lives then crediting therapy for the positive changes. You can collect bottle caps long enough to notice changes in your actions and then attribute those changes to bottle-cap collecting. With the advent of shorter-term therapies this ridiculousness remains apparent. To ignore a student's past is foolish. But to think you can explain or predict a student's current behavior by knowing that student's past is a mistake. People change over time. There is no fixed, unchanging personality that determines what you are or what you will become. Personality is only a shortcut to talking about what you have been doing recently.

8

On Feelings

Each year for more than thirty years I have flown to and from Japan twice, in spring and fall. I'm always scared when I fly, especially during turbulence. Often I tell people that my fear of flying is a kind of membership card, evidence that I understand their personal terror in phobic moments. But there are other reasons why I do not wish to be relieved of my fear of flying. Before I board a plane I am reminded to take an inventory of my life, as I'm expecting it to end during that flight. When I lived in Los Angeles for over thirty years I remember going to nearby Disneyland only once, thinking that I could go there anytime. But when I think of the morrow's flight, potentially my last, I pay more attention to my world. I live more "lifefully"—with sharpened senses and appreciation.

An upcoming flight gives me occasion to put my affairs in order. I leave instructions about what to do with my manuscripts, library, and other objects I have borrowed from life. I am privileged to tidy up my life over and over again, to compare the consistency and changes in my priorities over time. I say what needs to be said because it may be the last chance to communicate what is on my mind, in my heart. It is helpful to use one's very shinkiness and fear of death to accomplish important life tasks. While fearing to die, get your will written, finish letters and teaching activities and carpentry projects, and say what needs to be said to your loved ones.

Yet another reason my fear is a worthy mentor is that I know, really know, that my feelings are not my master. Feelings are real; they are sometimes strong. But I don't let them push me around. Afraid though I am, nevertheless I board the airplane. Feelings are not the whole of reality, not even the most important part of it and me. Feelings bring me messages, but so do friends and oncoming cars and maps and books and rosebushes and computers and music and many other representatives of reality. My flying while afraid keeps my feelings in their proper place, preventing them from getting out of hand. They do not dominate my life.

The feelings of anxiety and fear and worry are subjective feelings. Strictly speaking, these feelings cannot be compared among people. My experience of anxiety is my experience alone. The level of my anxiety cannot be compared with the level of yours. Scientists may try to measure these levels indirectly by means of various tests, but there is no way of knowing if what the tests measure is an accurate indication of comparable levels of experienced anxiety. This matter is important, because people will frequently explain their behavior in terms of their level of anxiety, fear, worry, or some other feeling state. You will hear people say that they don't fly because they are afraid of flying, that they can't drive on a freeway or give a speech in front of others because of their extreme fears. We cannot calculate the objective temperature when someone says they feel cold.

In CL we talk about feeling feelings and going ahead with constructive behavior in spite of them. Some students will then retort that our fears are weaker than theirs. Some psychotherapists will also claim that CL works well only for clients with lower levels of anxiety, fear, and other unpleasant feelings. Frankly, I question those assumptions. There is no way to compare my fear of flying with someone else's. I fly. Sometimes terrified, I fly. Whether or not one flies is *not* a valid measure of one's level of fear. It is a measure only of whether or not one flies. Bankei, in ancient Japan, told audiences that they were wasting their time in trying to eliminate thoughts and fearful feelings. Such efforts were like trying to "wash away blood with blood." In CL we use distraction to offer temporary relief from upsetting emotions. When utilizing the distraction "Band-Aid," it is not that while we are distracted those feelings are still continuing but we aren't noticing them, it is rather that the feelings are gone altogether, only to be regenerated when some new circumstance appears, such as stopping the distracting behavior or, in the case of fear of flying, when the plane hits turbulence. A study conducted by Herta Flor and colleagues at the University of Heidelberg's Central Institute of Mental Health found that spouses actually increased the degree of pain their partners felt by being overly sympathetic and solicitous. In contrast, spouses who distracted their partners without dwelling on the topic of their pain did not increase the neural activity associated with pain in their partner's brain.

One of my students remarked that she believes I am a doing person and she is a feeling person. But feelings are important to me too. It happens that right now as I write these lines I am in pain caused by my gastrointestinal system, and those feelings are VERY important, I assure you. Nevertheless, I can feel miserable and still be satisfied with the day because I got something accomplished. You may argue that it is impossible to get anything done feeling as terrible as you feel at a certain moment. The way to check out the validity of my statement is to accomplish something while you are feeling miserable and see if there is an improvement in your level of satisfaction.

Our society is rife with misconceptions about feelings/emotions. Here is an advertisement that exhibits a common misunderstanding about emotions: "CD-ROM Training to control emotions, sell more. . . . [This program] is designed for people who want to break destructive emotional habits such as anger, frustration, or anxiety. It also teaches how to manage one's feelings and situations that trigger negative reactions and keep one from performing at one's best."

Don't be fooled by this promise. Emotions aren't controlled or managed, behavior is. Emotions happen to us. Another misunderstanding is reflected in the following: "Thank you for your patience," says the automated telephone voice as I wait on the line. The voice should thank me for waiting (behavior), not for my patience (a feeling

I can't control). For that matter, I may not be feeling patient at all as I must wait for a live human voice to come on the line. Patience is not something that exists outside in the world. It is a shortcut to talking about whether a person is waiting with a certain feeling or not. You cannot cut open the brain or perform an fMRI on it and find a place where patience is located in any given moment.

The attempt to be happy *all* the time is patently silly. Consider the unrealistic situations in which people would try to be happy when a fire starts in their room or at their parent's funeral. Feelings fit circumstances. We should be flexible, accepting sorrow and grief as well as excitement and joy when they come. You are the one to decide what needs to be done in your life. Nobody else has that right. But don't get caught in the trap of trying to make yourself feel good about yourself or be happy *all* the time.

Dear Ann Landers:

I am tired of hearing and reading about people with cancer—how brave, courageous, noble and gallant they are. Often they are described as "heroic." Such flowery language might appeal to those who are seeking martyr status, but it's a real turnoff for me.

We who have cancer simply do what we have to do. We have no choice. We are not brave or courageous. We are scared to death, but we are realistic. We cling to anything to keep us afloat.

My daughter, at the age of thirty, was diagnosed with terminal bone cancer. I wasn't brave or courageous. I found that a heart can actually break. But I did what people in my place have always done. I decided I had to keep my head on straight and take care of her.

A year ago, I had a breast removed because of cancer. I am neither brave nor courageous, but again I am doing what I have to do, just as millions of others with cancer are doing. The world is every bit as beautiful as it was before I became

On Feelings

ill. I still have the love of friends and family. Every day counted before cancer, and every day counts now. I never thought of death as an enemy or that my pain and sorrow were a special cross I alone carried.

It is embarrassing to have friends and relatives tell me how brave I am and that they don't know how I do it. I want them to know I am one of millions who are doing the only thing we can do, and that is keep going. (TENNESSEE, Saturday, April 9, 1994; *The World,* Coos Bay, Ore., p. 15)

These days a number of strategies for dealing with mental health recommend accepting your feelings as they are. Meditation may help you sit with your feelings. Psychoanalysis may help you recognize and understand and accept your feelings. Constructive Living also recommends that you accept feelings as part of the reality that appears to you; but you are missing something if you don't move on to the next steps of knowing your purpose and doing what needs to be done. Reality won't allow you to be satisfied with acceptance alone. The acceptance of feelings and thoughts and situations is only a precursive step to realistic action.

Accepting feelings is part of the larger issue of accepting reality as it is. Cold *is.* Wishing it were warm does nothing to the temperature around us. Unless we take some action to affect it the cold remains until it is ready to go away. Feelings, too. Morning comes when it comes; storms hit us when they hit us; dropped dishes fall. Reality is as it is.

Here are some facts about feelings.

Feelings are real. "Unfelt feelings" is a meaningless pair of words, an oxymoron. No one has hidden feelings of which they are not aware. We have traces of feeling-related neural activity stored in our brains. These traces can evoke memories of feelings when stimulated. Precise feelings cannot be repeated, though similar ones are possible. Put another way, memory analogs seem to be stored in the brain. Triggered memories may evoke feelings, but the feelings are always new—reminders of past feelings, perhaps, but always different from those past feelings. The nervous system keeps changing, so feelings must change too.

Feelings abate over time as a result of broader experiences and decreased attempts to control or focus on them. Feelings increase when stimulated and when we try to control or suppress them. Being happy and anxiety-free all the time isn't useful or adaptive. We can't achieve and don't need continuous peace of mind. We need flexible minds, minds that respond to real circumstances realistically.

Anxiety reflects desires—the greater the desire the more anxious we become if the desire isn't satisfied. For example, the more we want to succeed on an exam the more tension we feel until we get a good result. The CL sense of understanding anxiety is in accepting its existence as part of reality, not fathoming its origins or analyzing its components.

- Fear gives us information. It warns us to be careful on a dark street; it prompts caution. Fear is a cue about a problem in the environment; something needs doing.
- Sorrow is natural after loss and even before anticipated loss.
- Lack of confidence signals insufficient risk, insufficient success, and insufficient experience.
- Happiness involves temporarily losing the self—in things, humor, service, work, meditation, others, etc.
- Misery involves extreme self-focus and so increases during any psychotherapy that is self- and feeling-focused.
- Feelings, like advice, give us information, but they are not the only source of information for selecting behavior. It is better to work on controllable behavior than on uncontrollable feelings.
- We cannot eliminate desires—including the desire to eliminate desires. Furthermore, we don't need to do so. Desires provide the opportunity for satisfaction too. What we need to do is eliminate the singular power that desires have over our lives.

On Feelings

We will all suffer; we will all experience misery. We can eliminate the suffering on top of suffering caused by unrealistically trying to eliminate suffering directly.

These laws of feeling in Constructive Living are absolute, like gravity. They are descriptions of the way feelings are observed to operate. You can believe in gravity or not, but it will still go on operating in its naturally lawful ways. And, of course, as new circumstances appear with new information we can modify and refine our CL understanding of those laws about feeling.

Guilt, too, is a natural feeling phenomenon; it need not be worked on or eliminated. I once met a patient who was in psychotherapy working on the guilt he felt about keeping his mother in a nursing home even though she didn't need to be there. It seemed to me that his guilt wasn't pathological but a normal indicator of what needed to be done—allow his mother to return to his home. Guilt, like all feelings, gives us information about what needs doing. What one does with that information will affect how long the feeling continues to be experienced. For example, guilt may prompt you to repay your parents, but how you make efforts to repay them is the key to responding to ("dealing with") the guilt.

The feeling focus of modern culture masks laziness, sloppy thinking, rationalization, and self-indulgence. I doubt that there was a time in human history when many people didn't recognize what they were feeling, but now there is an overemphasis on feelings as the most important element of human life. Some people seem to be attending primarily to their own feelings, building their lives around them. As noted above, the need these days is not to get in touch with feelings, but to get in touch with the reality of circumstances.

Constructive Living doesn't ask anyone to give up feeling. However, we must beware of overindulging the feeling side of our lives. When we focus on emotions exclusively other important aspects of living are neglected. We must balance our awareness of feelings with attentive, purposeful action in the world.

Back in the 1970s voices were raised in protest against the uncritical acceptance of the theory that it is unhealthy to bottle up feelings, that aggression must be expressed openly. Careful research results showed that expressing aggression, even in supposedly "safe" settings like therapy, could lead to even more aggression in other settings. It is not simply a case of "getting out" some bottled aggression once and for all. Rewarding even verbal aggression encourages a person to attack others verbally in other situations. This spillover effect makes any therapy that encourages direct display of destructive behavior dangerous, whatever the fine intentions of the therapists. As you must see by now, Constructive Living recommends accepting our feelings for what they are and then getting on with doing what needs doing.

In her book on growing up black in Bennettsville, South Carolina, *The Measure of Our Success,* Marian Edelman wrote: "Giving up and 'burnout' were not part of the language of my elders—you got up every morning and you did what you had to do and you got up every time you fell down and tried as many times as you had to to get it done right."

This wisdom is not confined to any race or culture or time period.

9

In Praise of Pain

I couldn't have written this chapter three weeks ago. I was hurting too much then. My left side ached, my intestines burned, my stomach threatened anything I sent its way. I was weak, disoriented, and exhausted by months of misery and medical tests that didn't reveal the source of the disease. Standing up brought some relief. Sitting and lying down were torture. Hope and despair twirled together in a grotesque dance I no longer cared to view.

Waiting requires attention and effort for me. I like getting things done, cleared up, out of the way. I was eager for medication, examinations, even surgery, anything to get past the ambiguity and pain. What was the difference if the procedures produced more pain, even intense pain? The closure would be worth it. Whatever it was, the disease didn't appear to be life-threatening. No one seemed to know what to do about it. Wait. Endure. Try this painkiller and this stomach-acid neutralizer. More medication for side effects. Get done what you can.

I'm not suggesting that pain is wonderful—it's too close as I write to consider that true—but, like fire, it is useful: dangerous, requiring careful attention; basic, without substitute.

Pain admitted me to membership in the group whose members share a bond of intensely private bodily suffering. It caused me to reorient my priorities and meanings in life. It guided me to be less concerned with my appearance. It spurred me to repay debts and prepare for death. It caused me to look more closely at the details of my daily life. . . .

Now, much later, the pain has diminished somewhat. This body has worked to heal itself. No longer on medication, I have discovered home remedies (such as mint chewing gum) when the discomfort interferes with necessary tasks. Nevertheless, I still identify with those who are sitting in doctors' office waiting rooms and lying in hospital beds. I no longer pass such places casually with the thought that they are unrelated to my existence. I understand the churning emotions of fear and hope and distress and despair, the insistent self-focus, the shredded pride, the sense of bodily betrayal, the worry about when the pain will come back again, the concern with the side effects of the medicine. Pain has helped me to embrace more of the human race— those who are suffering in pain right now and those who suffered in the past.

We don't want to look closely at death and cancer and AIDS and poverty and grief in real life. We can stand it when they are distanced by newsprint or monitors and television screens. We make efforts to avoid reminders of our own mortality and impotence. Of course, some of us have the choice, much of the time, of ignoring those aspects of reality that make us uncomfortable. Sometimes, however, illness and pain, death and disaster, demand our attention anyway. Reality intrudes on the protected fictions of our lives. In those moments we discover who we really are. In those moments we have the opportunity to make fundamental changes in our identities.

Nonetheless, I wish you many peaceful moments free from pain.

In Praise of Pain

10

Whirling Dust

How much of modern life is the equivalent of studying outdated television listings, listening to recordings of last week's traffic and weather reports, clipping expired coupons from yellowed newspapers? How much of modern life is just allowing information to flow through, filling our mental time? (We'll consider the possibility of procrastination in a moment.) What is the clear purpose in reading a newspaper or watching a commercial on television? When did modern life begin to be replete with word laxatives, swallowed and, well, passed— smoothly, effortlessly passed? Did it begin with advertising? With marketing decisions that fed us slick, soft slop? Not altogether; why blame others? When did we begin to slurp our mental soup?

Many people appear to prefer to go on gathering more information than act on the information they already possess. Now I have no objection to gathering information, of course. However, the gathering of data from the media every day can continue to the degree that life's term papers never get written. We can flood ourselves with masses of information into a state of immobility. We must know our purposes. If our data gathering is aimed at putting off necessary action, we must shift gears. I am disturbed by the thoughtless pace of communications in our time. To be sure, there is a time to use tweeting, e-mail, fax, phone, and overnight mail. But too often it seems that people use those modes of communication because they simply haven't planned ahead or because they have become accustomed to using them, needed or not.

We are all going to die. That fact is the foundation on which our lives should be built. At reality's pace in reality's time we shall die, are dying right now. There are occasions when reality opens a brief window of opportunity, and we must act quickly. Nevertheless, with some foresight and thoughtful scheduling we can provide ourselves with enough time to do our communicating well, not merely fast. I am not foolish enough to suggest that we go back to reliance on hand-delivered messages and smoke signals in this modern age. But there is need for thoughtful, well-considered communications in any age.

Those who receive our messages deserve to take in something well considered. They deserve to have time to ponder our meaning and offer a prudent response at their own pace. It is impolite and inconsiderate to ask for a prompt fax reply, an instant text return, or an immediate return call. Of course, sometimes circumstances prompt us to be impolite and inconsiderate, but not without deliberation about the inconvenience we are about to cause others.

For many of us life is so easy. Some depressed people spend long hours in bed trying to kill time by remaining unconscious. They see themselves as having nothing meaningful to do with all the time their lives offer them. Modern technology frees us from many routine tasks. What are we to do with that free time? Purposeful tasks were always right before the eyes of those living a hundred years ago, for they were intimately connected to the daily needs for food, shelter, clothing, and so forth. In modern times many of us have unprecedented leisure, wealth, and resources. We take vacations, sick leave, and holidays, and we retire. We are faced with a new challenge in this era—how to use our time purposefully, meaningfully.

In the absence of other clear purposes some people turn their attention to their bodies, focusing on every slight change they sense in them. They worry about their health constantly. They overmedicate themselves. They obsess about health foods, health fads, and health clubs. Others find narrow purpose in building financial security or financial empires. Still others flit from partner to partner seeking meaning in temporary liaisons. However we value or disvalue these pursuits, they provide purposes, objectives, and goals for attention, thinking, and behavior.

It is important for all of us to keep our moment-by-moment purposes clear. What is my purpose in writing this book? What is my purpose in standing rather than sitting before this keyboard? What is my purpose in wearing these particular clothes now? What is my purpose in picking up or not picking up that magazine?

I am told that guidance counselors in schools are taught to search out the underlying psychological causes of study problems rather than teaching effective study techniques. If that is so, it would explain some of the decline in educational achievement in American youth. Even if the counselors were to discover the psychological problems, no one knows how to solve them, so they become mere rationales or excuses for failure. Recently, Japanese teachers have been instructed to instill self-confidence and self-esteem in their students. Japanese education, too, will decline as the emphasis shifts toward doing the impossible and unnecessary.

On the one hand, kids get parenting for free, so they may not value it. On the other hand, busy earning money, many Americans appear to want to relinquish their responsibility for rearing their own children. They have turned over to schoolteachers, counselors, and child psychologists the joys and frustrations of raising them. The result is that something valuable has been taken from all of us and hidden behind doors of accepted custom, locked by pseudo-science. You can reclaim your real treasure by simply acting with worthy purpose.

The trend these days is to do what is right but avoid the consequences of proper action. However, it may be necessary to pay a price for such righteousness. We must be willing to do so. Don't get the idea that watching a television program (about diving or arguing or catching criminals or running an organization, for example) is the same as experiencing those activities yourself.

As we rush impatiently through life, there are many moments when we may thoughtlessly waste time. What do you do while your computer is warming up? What do you do as you wait for an Internet connection or download? While you wait for copies to emerge from the machine, or while you are on hold on the telephone, or while your car engine is warming up, or while your spouse is dressing, or while the commercial is on your television screen—what are you doing and where is your mind? These short blocks of time can be put to good use if you are prepared and alert.

Reflections on Mind

The West holds that you can understand the "it" that blinks your eyes and opens your mouth and raises your hand. The East holds that this "it" cannot be understood but that it is constantly experienced. The person who hasn't given the matter much thought is unaware even of the existence of an "it." To say that "I" blink and "I" speak and "I" raise my hand seems to take care of the matter for most people. Some people even confuse mind and brain. However, the mind is not the brain, though the two are clearly related in some complex fashion. The mind has no location in space. I can point to your brain but not to your mind.

It is not at all that there is a mind in which thoughts and feelings arise. Rather, those thoughts and feelings *are* the mind. Dr. Shinichi Usa points out that the mind is like a television program with only one channel. So it is with mental suffering; one cannot erase anxiety from the mind and have a mind left over in that moment. Similarly, it is not that I have a creative mind that makes up original ideas. Sometimes I am in touch with the creative spirit, though it isn't *my* creative spirit. Whose it is remains unspecifiable and immaterial. It is available to anyone. Creating is not something I do but something that happens to me. Sometimes it becomes me. There are times when we process information but aren't aware of the information source or the processing mode. We come to conclusions without knowing the means by which we reached those conclusions. Such would be a satisfactory definition of "intuition." But isn't all our mental life like that? We operate on intuition all the time, except that we have learned satisfactory "stories" about the means by which we draw conclusions and form purposes and plans of action. Just as nobody knows why anyone does what he/she does, so nobody knows how we arrive at conclusions, interpretations, purposes, and understandings. They, too, happen to us.

Do you think you could do a complete study of a magnifying glass using only that magnifying glass itself? You need to look through it at something else in order to discover some of its merits and flaws. You need other instruments, even other magnifying glasses, to study it further. It is the same with the mind. In the study of our own minds (through meditation, for example) the instrument of study and the object of study are the same. The results are already colored by the instrument we use. This relativity of self-understanding cannot be escaped. We cannot step outside ourselves to understand ourselves. So it is a *good idea* to use a variety of instruments to examine ourselves in order to reduce some of the biases built into our mind-instrument. Reality provides useful information if we *pay attention* to it. The problem lies in whether or not reality is just another name for our mind-instrument.

The intellectual mind likes regularity and order. The neurotic mind likes familiarity, even if that familiarity is painful. The modern mind likes change and bright lights. Perhaps my emphasis on the simplifying function of the mind lies in my own need to simplify when I present CL ideas in the Japanese language or to media people in the United States. In a way, the mind is like an ox. It must be tamed and trained. In general, Japanese are better at controlling their minds. Thus they have better-behaved minds. On the other hand, American minds are more creative, challenging assumptions. The ideal mind would be both well-behaved and creative. Dr. Shinichi Usa points out that trying to polish the mind is like trying to polish a television program that is always in motion.

Attention

Neurosis is a matter of attention. The more one focuses attention on the suffering—noticing how unpleasant it is, trying to get rid of it, wishing it didn't exist, comparing the self with others who don't appear to suffer in this way, worrying about when the suffering will appear next, emphasizing other difficulties related to it, complaining that it is greater than one deserves and than can be endured, and so on—the more one's attention is diverted from everyday tasks, responsibilities, and joys.

A Japanese physician who specializes in the treatment of *katakori* or stiff-shoulder syndrome, a common malady in Japan, believes that over-attention paid to the shoulder muscles helps to bring on and sustain the problem. Particular attention to a body part may have some effect on the blood flow to that area or some other physiological effect that results in the experiencing of discomfort. Morita wrote about a vicious cycle of attention and sensitivity in psychological areas (such as social tensions, fear of blushing, and so forth). I wonder if that principle could not be generalized to psychophysiological problems as well. If so, there would be a therapeutic advantage to displacing the attention to more constructive areas. We know that action involving large muscles draws attention, so physical exercise, manual labor, dance, and other activities requiring movement could be therapeutic for nonspecific shoulder tension, stomach problems, headaches, back pain—and neurotic rumination, too.

After a couple of days of pulling weeds from the garden on Kauai, I begin to see weeds everywhere—when visiting neighbors, when out hiking, and so forth. There is a time to focus on weeds and a time to focus on flowers, however. It is a matter of paying attention. Note that the Viagra boom took place because after trials of the drug as a heart medicine some of the subjects were reluctant to give it back. Someone *noticed* this phenomenon and discovered that those subjects had experienced better sexual functioning through use of the drug. Paying attention paid off.

13

Paralysis by Possibility—
Unipossible and Multipossible Situations

Unipossible situations are those in which only a single option is perceived to be available. The choice is whether to accept the option or reject it. Multipossible situations offer more than one option. Extreme multipossible situations with many options may make an individual feel paralyzed, unable to select from among the possibilities. For example, common extreme multipossible situations may occur shortly after retirement, after winning a lottery, with sudden fame, and so forth.

It can be argued that the natural tendency of most humans is to avoid extreme multipossible situations. The routine of going to a regular job at a regular time reduces perceived choices and thus eliminates the need for conscious evaluation and decision making at certain times. I have argued elsewhere that one of the functions of paranoia (everything is seen as threatening, dangerous), love (the loved one matters to the exclusion of others), and drugs (obtaining drugs and using them become the prime activity) is to simplify choices, to reduce perceived multipossible situations to unipossible ones. Simplifying one's life is a common priority for all of us. However, the ways in which we simplify it and the things we decide to eliminate are important. Take, for example, a bookshelf filled with many unread books compared with one holding only one or two unread books. Selection is quite a different matter in these two cases.

As further examples, monastic Christianity and monastic Buddhism serve to reduce stimuli and perceived choices for monks.

It can be said that many aspects of culture—laws, economics, government—are designed to aid the members of that culture to reduce the number of choices available to them. Science, too, offers reduced options to scientists and others.

One can imagine a future in which it will take all day to plan the menu, decide when and where to sleep, or select clothing for the day because there will be so many possibilities. The mind becomes cluttered, like a disorderly desktop with more and more added to the pile on top. One of the advantages of driving a car for long distances in silence is that one's ideas shake down, get organized, even disappear. The mind becomes less cluttered. Becoming lost in one's present activity is another way of temporarily putting aside the extra mental baggage we carry around. At some point we wake up and shoulder the baggage again, then lose ourselves in reality's tasks, then return to the baggage—over and over.

There are so many of us human beings. On television we can turn those others off, play them back, or skip their shows altogether. Yet every time we turn on the set they reappear, with their contrived enthusiasm and their screen-thin smiles. They stand in our way at sports events and delay our progress in supermarket checkout lines. It is necessary to get away from them—all of them—once in a while. The river that churns beside me here and now has no sensitive feelings that can be hurt, no endless words, no neediness. It just flows. In the process of flowing it cools and wears down rocks and feeds life and opens the land. Strange that with the passing of time I will want to go back to the city.

One reason why reading books has the advantage over watching ordinary television programming is less in the programs' content (there are some fine documentaries and thought-provoking dramas on television), but in the fact that live television is happening in real time, so you have no time to stop and ponder before the next event occurs. A book always waits while you pause for thought. Television can be more usefully watched on video recorder, so that the viewer can stop the program at any time and think.

Paralysis by Possibility

14

Under New Management

Control by means of understanding was one of the central contributions of the ancient Greeks. The better humans understood something, the better we could manage it—that was the idea. Such an approach works quite well with cars and chemicals and rockets and computers. It isn't so effective with minds. Understanding your mind very well doesn't allow you to control it. Insight doesn't necessarily produce peace of mind or orderly, purpose-filled behavior. The Japanese psychiatrist Morita suggested that we have a better chance of achieving peace of mind by accepting it as it is rather than attempting to control it by in-depth understanding. Let go and accept your feelings and doubts and ideals, he suggested. In the meantime act purposefully, do what is right. So Morita's therapy was about controlling one's own behavior, not about figuring everything out psychologically. Attempting to understand the mind with the mind is rather like trying to pull oneself up by one's own bootstraps.

It is important to understand what is controllable and what is not controllable in life. At a training session one young man remarked to me, "Because I couldn't control my anger I blew up." Wrong! At the time he wasn't clear on what is controllable and what is not. His anger was uncontrollable. Such is the case for everyone. Blowing up is behavior. Behavior can and should be monitored and controlled. We are responsible for what we do precisely because behavior is controllable. Anger alone didn't cause the young man to blow up; it was laziness and poor habits and his relinquishment of managing his behavior. Some people fail to make this distinction between feelings and behavior. They think that anger and blowing up are the same thing. They are not. Anger occurs within the mind; it is a feeling. Blowing up is an action. It can be seen by others, manifests itself in such actions as shouting or throwing things or stomping out of the room. Confusion in this area causes both psychological and social problems.

Have you ever seen the ox-herding paintings from Japan? They are a set of (usually) ten simple black-ink paintings depicting a young lad searching for his ox, finding it, disciplining it, leading it, riding on it, and then turning it loose. (There is more to the story that doesn't concern us here.) One interpretation of the series is that it represents a metaphorical tale of the control of one's body. The body is like an ox in that we must search for the proper means of managing it, train it until desired behaviors become habits, and then enjoy the fruits of our self-discipline. In order to improvise well, all musicians must first master their instruments. Behavioral habits accumulated over time become character.

"It is never too late to be what you might have been" (George Eliot).

15

Contentment

How does one go about determining when one is content, or miserable, or just doing all right? When does one reach a point at which one believes some action is necessary to change dissatisfaction?

I began to grapple with these questions as a result of several studies in the first few years of my postdoctoral research. One study involved assessing the motivations for suicide. Sometimes it appeared that fairly common setbacks or minor irritations precipitated suicidal behaviors. Another study involved neurotic Japanese young people who seemed to be suffering terribly from relatively commonplace adolescent shyness and feelings of self-doubt.

Looking within myself, I too could find similar negative experiences and feelings. Yet I considered them only minor chords in a larger and more positive life melody. What made the difference? Why do the same sorts of problems lead to suicide in some people and not in others?

At the upper end of the emotional spectrum, certainly, continuous euphoria is hard to sustain. Even when chemically induced there are problems of habituation, increasing psychological sensitivity thresholds to discomfort, and the practical difficulties of maintaining the supply of prescribed happiness. At the other end of the spectrum I suspect that there are some woes and miseries that we could all pretty much agree are such that they produce dissatisfaction, unhappiness, or despondency.

Yet in between those end points how wide are our individual ranges of satisfaction and dissatisfaction? How broad is that intermediate range of feelings and experiences that we define as neither particularly pleasant nor unpleasant? How do I learn to evaluate, for example, the sense I have when I drift off along tangential paths of thought in the midst of writing this piece—pleasant or unpleasant? When is being alone pleasant and when unpleasant? How do I know when I am "fulfilling myself?" When I am "doing what needs doing" is that supposed to make me happy or satisfied or what?

Some minds have a tendency to acknowledge life by feeling extremely good or suffering terribly. Those minds require life to be lived at the extremes of emotion. In the midst of making love or receiving applause or achieving some cherished goal, who hasn't wished that the moment might go on and on? Who hasn't regretted that this particular now must be replaced by other less glorious nows?

Contentment

77

16

Backups, Throwaway Tissues, Road Kill, and Resources—Self-focus in America

In the grim interpersonal sense, backups are people we keep in reserve to use when times get rough. They may be parents, children, lovers, friends, or anyone else on whom we can impose. We are likely to contact them when we need something from them. Tissues are people whom we have used and thrown away. They may be people from whom we borrowed money, people who hired us or taught us and are no longer useful. We forget about them and the contributions they made to our lives so that we can avoid thoughts of indebtedness or repayment. Road kill are people who got in our way as we moved toward success. They may be families, supervisors, spouses, lovers, siblings, friends, classmates, or others. We push them aside as soon as we see that they would interfere with our achieving our goals.

The common feature of these categories is the selfishness on which the interactions are based. There is no concern for the convenience of the others, just with our own needs and goals. Furthermore, be careful when considering people as "resources," even as resources for others. People cannot be reduced to the single facet of "resource." One effect of urban life is that, for some, people have become mere props and scenery rather than human characters in their electronic life plays. Urban circuitry produces plugged-in people. It is no longer a boy and his dog, but a man and his computer; no longer a girl and her girlfriends, but a woman and her smart phone.

Capitalism requires that both the consumer and the producer

have self-interest. Theory says these self-serving needs should balance each other. Capitalism is based on the realistic premise that all of us are sinners in the sense of ordinarily putting our own convenience first. In this strange world, worth is measured by the ability to consume. You can assure yourself of respected treatment if you are a customer—particularly if you are interested in the top-of-the-line product. Those who are labeled "shopaholics" may indeed be trying to build self-worth through their excessive purchasing.

As a country grows prosperous, the lives of the individual citizens are no longer tied to the real necessities of making an everyday living. They begin to drift from reality-based living into abstract, word-based living. They become more susceptible to religious leaders and pop-psych gurus who talk a good line and to politicians who make grand promises. No matter how much we have we are still likely to go after new purposes, challenges, unknowns—all the while risking potential danger. Desires always outreach attainments.

Our present emphasis on the fast pace, the quick comeback, the snappy reply, causes us to live closer to spontaneity, diminishing our interest in evaluation and control, thus leading to more irrationality and social problems. We live as though we were fast-forwarding through a video of a tea ceremony.

Dealing with a problem compassionately and rationally is a wonderful human activity. Those who abuse drugs and alcohol, the elderly, the dying, suffering neurotics, and others all need our compassionate and sensible help. Our culture seems to be defining such help as the exclusive province of medicine. Of course, compassionate support may be medical, but it is not necessarily so. If we begin to equate benevolent support with medical support alone, we are in trouble for a variety of reasons, not least of which is the fact that medical support is gradually being weaned from compassion to economics, from caregiving to profitmaking. Of course, not all physicians or nurses or medical support people are caught up in this trend. But it is dangerous to put all our compassion eggs in a basket that has become less than sturdy.

Backups, Throwaway Tissues, Road Kill, and Resources

In *The World* for February 20, 1994, Norm Russell wrote that on a special episode of the television program *Night Line* a panelist stated: "As a society, Americans have become much more comfortable in saying someone is sick or that they are suffering from this complex or this syndrome than we are saying that someone has done something bad or evil. We have abolished sin, we've medicalized it." He went on to point out: "No one does anything wrong anymore, they are sick. No one is held responsible for their conduct, they are victims. No one commits sin anymore, they are suffering from some complex."

17

On Being Natural

I wonder whether most Americans want to hear the fact that, however much we may wish to be extraordinary, nearly all of the time we are unremarkable. American culture seems to place a strong positive value on individuality, diversity, and unconventionality. Look at the synonyms for "ordinary" in a dictionary or thesaurus. The great majority of them have negative connotations—"commonplace," "bland," "stale," "banal," "trite," "dull," and "prosaic" being typical examples. But "ordinary" need not be negative. It also contains the potential for security, regularity, peace, and even for normal growth and development. There is nothing wrong with going for the gold, but such efforts must begin with a realistic understanding of our ordinary human limitations and potential. How can anyone bound in the chains of status and fame speak or write about the ordinary life?

Who doesn't grow nervous in the presence of a new sweetheart? Who doesn't feel anxiety before a job interview? Television, for example, has produced new ideals, impossibly high standards. Viewers don't ordinarily see the outtakes, the errors, the stumbling, the forgotten lines, and the tension of announcers waiting to be on camera. The cool, smooth delivery of television announcers and screen actors would be artificial in many everyday life circumstances. Don't seek the impossible; do what you can; accept the discrepancy.

"Don't hang around kings, important officials, powerful people, or people full of lust and eager for name and fame, or tellers of tales. . . .

Don't take delight in crowds or seek for disciples. Don't study or practice too many things. . . . Green waters and verdant mountains are the place to walk in meditation; by the streams, under the trees are places to clear the mind" (Cleary, 1980, p. 117, quoted from Keizan Jokin's *Zazen Yojinki*). This wise man is recommending that we take a stroll out-of-doors to remind ourselves of our fundamental place in nature. While head-tripping in the soft glow of a television screen we can momentarily lose our roots. Beware!

18

Some Truths

First, here are some truths about life and death.

We will all die. We will leave all we have worked for—things, creations, people, reputation, etc.

Others will be living when we die.

Some trees and other elements of nature will outlive us.

Our names and historical reputations will be no more than ideas that will change and disappear after our deaths.

Suffering interferes with our noticing/enjoying/appreciating some aspects of life.

We will encounter barriers and limitations to accomplishing our goals.

The problem with suicide is that we cannot try other life solutions after we are dead.

Second, here are some truths about neurotic suffering.

Words and intellectual knowledge alone will not eliminate neurotic suffering.

Neurotic suffering is neither good nor bad.

Neurotic suffering is momentary, not endless.

Neurotic suffering is unrelated to logic.

Neurotic suffering need not prevent you from living a full life.

Neurotic suffering is real suffering, not imagined suffering.

Nobody else can understand your neurotic suffering.

No one else can repair your neurotic suffering.

Neurotic suffering has a positive source, if you want to look for it.

Neurotic suffering cannot be explained by brain scans, chemicals, past history, personality, or any other mode of reasonable explanation.

19

Reflections on Interpersonal Relations

I don't claim to have any special expertise in interpersonal relations. I have misunderstood and wronged enough people to know how lacking in skill I can be at times. Nevertheless, from seventy-odd years of experience living in two cultures and operating in two languages I can pass along some very basic observations about us humans.

On Love

Being in love won't get the dishes washed or the lawn mowed.

Sometimes you have to sleep alone.

When we are in love we try to be the best person for our loved one. Part of the joy of being in love is being at our best.

Who wants a casual lover with diarrhea? Casual lovers are for convenience, not commitment. A measure of genuine love is the degree of trouble one partner is gladly willing to go to for the other. Going to such trouble may actually create more love in both parties.

With regard to jealousy, it isn't just the sex given to another lover that we begrudge; it's the attention. Even that attention alone, without any physical contact, is coveted.

How inconsiderate is the luxury of love! It disappears with a paper cut or garden work or a full bladder.

Expressing love doesn't make the feeling go away. Saying "I love you" doesn't bring that feeling out in the open and eliminate it.

Expressing a feeling may enhance it.

One of the simplifying filters of life is love. It is not necessary to please everyone as long as the loved one is pleased.

When lovers are separated for long periods of time they become ideas, icons in each other's minds. The experience of separation may lead one to realize that, even when together, we are ideas and icons in the mind of our lovers.

On Quarreling

Quarrels can be seen as presenting problems to be solved, a sort of *koan* puzzle for the couple. When there is a quarrel and the couple finds a solution without breaking up, they are encouraged about the strength of their commitment to each other.

Be prepared to stop when your partner's warning lights flash.

What does "winning" an argument mean? It can mean stopping the fight with an apology. In that case the apology is the controlling factor in putting a stop to the argument. The person who apologizes first wins.

We take our partner's good points and efforts in our behalf for granted and wish for that small thing they won't give us.

When I complain to myself that she doesn't see the situation the way I do it is always a sign that I don't see the situation as she does.

On Marriage

Marriage is an institution designed to allow the marriage partners to serve each other. Most people find fewer opportunities to serve others when living alone.

What can you give someone when all they want from you is more space? Answer: Love and space.

Humans, in order to avoid lonely moments, surround themselves with those who love and respect them, or at least those who recognize them. It is hard being a stranger.

Water, Snow, Water

Humans want their mates to offer them symbolic sacrifices. Men and women will push to test the limits of their partners' patience. However, they rarely persist in their testing if they are permitted to transgress occasionally and are held accountable for overstepping the bounds. Even when we believe we have gotten away with something we humans exhibit a sort of compulsion to confess—to cleanse ourselves of memories and secrets from the past, to hurt the beloved other, and to check to see if we are still loved despite our breach of limits.

Some spouses think that they can dominate a marriage by working hard and serving their mate and then being righteous and idealistic about their own desires. At least they try to earn their power. But what such spouses don't realize is that all their efforts are gifts received from others, even the service itself. They don't see that even successful service causes trouble to people and things.

Successful marriage involves concern about the other's convenience, actual service, words of gratitude and affection and apology, and the blurring of roles.

Don't be obsessed by anything—including marriage. Marriage will not save you or give you security or end your selfishness or give meaning to your life.

Adapted from Ron Madson's "Advice for Spice (spouses)" (personal communication):

1. Create opportunities to make your partner look good.
2. Be respectful. Offer advice only when asked for it.
3. Change in yourself whatever you want changed in your partner. Give your partner what you want.
4. Proffer thanks and apologies appropriately and often.
5. Make decisions based on cooperation and shared purposes. Give in.
6. Perform romantic and loving deeds. Do first chores that your partner wants done. Plan special surprises and special events for your spouse.

John Gottman, head of the Family Formation Project at the University of Washington, has found that satisfied couples maintained a ratio of at least five positive moments to each negative moment during their interactions. Whether highly emotional or not, whether frequently fighting or avoiding conflicts, whether complaining or not, those couples who behave kindly toward one another at least those five times as often as not are likely to stay together. Partners don't need deep psychological insight into the presumed causes of their conflicts. They need to treat each other well. They need to behave with courtesy and consideration.

We don't live in order to marry. Prepare for a single life with friends, financial self-support, health, and practical living skills. If you do marry, then these attributes will be a plus; marry from strength, not weakness.

If your purpose is to find a life partner, don't wait for a prince or princess to appear at your door. Go to clubs and parks, volunteer, attend classes, travel. Have an accepting, open, eager-to-learn attitude.

Raising a child offers you the chance to learn how to give up your own convenience for the sake of that child. You also learn that sometimes you are helpless to solve a problem to your child's satisfaction. Furthermore, you learn to examine your own purposes and objectives in the light of this new family member.

Mother Love

There is a mother in Kyushu who made sketches of leaves together with her son and took walks with him during the period in which he refused to go to school. He eventually returned to school.

Another boy grew angry with his mother, complaining about the food she gave him. He ran out of the house and didn't come back until late that evening, when he found his place set at the table and his food waiting for him. Why is this response better than refusing to feed him his dinner in order to teach him a lesson?

Love's Expression

Love results in the magnification of feelings of all sorts. Jealousy, anger, abandonment, and so forth are all subjects for love's loupe.

Don't limit your expressions of love to hugging and endearing words. Here are some other possible ways to express it:

- Turning off a favorite television program in order to hear about your partner's day when he/she comes home.
- Interrupting your involvement in some engrossing task to see your partner off when he/she leaves home.
- Preparing food that your partner likes but you don't.
- Allowing your partner to do things for you.
- Speaking to your partner politely and courteously even when both of you are tired and upset.

Stages of Love

Stage 1. Discovering the partner's potential and gifts
Stage 2. Discovering the partner's limits and weaknesses
Stage 3. Accepting the partner as one accepts oneself—namely, as imperfect but nonetheless lovable

The Progression of Love Talk

Stage 1. We take romantic talk at face value.
Stage 2. We wonder why our mates keep repeating the same loving talk; we already know they love us.
Stage 3. We appreciate the intent and effort that underlie loving talk, however many times we have heard it.

Kind Criticism

There are times when it is necessary to convey negative or critical information to others we care about. We realize that to do so is to cause them trouble and perhaps to incite defensiveness and anger. Here are some practical methods for presenting negative information (e.g., a light was left on in the bathroom all night, your mate has bad breath, your spouse is getting fat, there is an alcohol problem) without criticizing, complaining, or nagging:

1. Criticize yourself for the same or a related problem.
2. Present it as a purposeful mistake or misunderstanding ("Thanks for leaving the light on for me, but I'm not ready to use the bathroom yet").
3. Offer a clever, imaginative expression of the problem to soften the criticism.
4. Joke about the quirk.
5. Refer to the desired or undesired behavior indirectly by talking about another person.
6. Ask a question related to the problem behavior.
7. Praise some past condition (e.g., "You looked so beautiful in your wedding dress").
8. Praise the desired behavior in someone else.
9. Surround the criticism with praise. Always offer much more praise than criticism.
10. Surround the criticism with sincerity and expressions of affection. Avoid sarcasm.
11. Offer a gift (such as a mint to someone with bad breath).
12. Offer education (such as a clipping with information about smoking or obesity).
13. Refer to the value changed behavior will have for someone else (e.g., "For the children's future . . .").
14. Refer to some shared, overriding purpose you both hold dear.
15. Emphasize how the desired behavior would be helpful to you (e.g., "Please do me a favor . . ."; "I would really appreciate your doing . . ."; "My work would be so much easier if you would . . .").
16. Offer to do something yourself (e.g., to leave the room if the smoker wishes to continue smoking, to wash the dirty cup on the counter).

Water, Snow, Water

17. Adopt the practice of thanking the other person when he/she criticizes your behavior.
18. Set aside a gentle "time-out" period for frank discussion of each other's undesired behaviors so that each partner can better please the other better.

Qualities That Generate Love

Openness, self-disclosure, expressions of love, working together toward shared goals, physical touching, generosity, humility, gratitude

Qualities That Stifle Love

Overexaggerated politeness, cruelty, propriety, obligations, competition, busyness, time constraints, self-centeredness, selfishness, self-protectiveness, pride

Random Thoughts

We all need moments of privacy. I recommend that when you and your loved one go to a party together you separate to talk to others and fill each other in afterward about what went on, that you sustain your grooming/appearance even when just the two of you are at home, that you keep bathroom views private, that you keep separate workplaces, and that you learn to enjoy some separate activities.

If you must leave a loved one, leave him/her better off than when you first got together. Give and give until you wave goodbye.

If I continue to insist on telling you what to do or what not to do, I devour you and I become a glutton.

Some people think that when they are engrossed in a task they are exempt from politely replying to anyone who interrupts them. They are wrong.

Let us consider the notion of "causing" pain to others. Suppose Mary breaks up with Fred and Fred feels grief. We assume that Mary caused Fred's pain. But consider a situation in which Fred has already found another girlfriend and has been waiting to reveal this information to Mary. In this case, when Mary breaks up with Fred he is not grief-stricken. Clearly, there must be some other circumstances in addition to Mary's action of breaking up to account for Fred's pain. Those conditions may include Fred's mood at the moment, social conditions (e.g., whether or not there is another woman in his life), how tired he is, how absorbed he is in that new project at work, and so forth. Mary doesn't control all those conditions and has no responsibility for them. Mary is responsible only for what Mary does. But she does have reasonable responsibility for knowing what is going on with Fred before she announces the breakup.

Do you think because someone has had an enlightenment experience, or because he is a respected educator or politician or clergyman, that he should never be attracted to a charming woman? If this were so, something valuable in life would be lost. What these males do about the attraction depends on the values of the parties involved, on what they consider should be done, on all sorts of conditions. But the attraction itself is natural.

I knew a man who worried about the possibility of his wife's committing suicide, not because of its effect on her, but because it would cause him trouble. Then, realizing this, he proceeded to worry about his own flawed ethics. Reflexive reflections.

You can kill another human being's desire to help by refusing the offer to help, by immediately correcting the helping action without acknowledging the intent to help behind it, or by criticizing the helping act itself. Even when you know you can do the job quicker and better yourself it may be best to accept help with thanks. It is important to recognize and reward the effort of another person even when the results are poor or undesirable.

For example, when a husband responded with concern for his wife she told him that he wasn't expressing his "true" feelings. Because these words made him angry, he sarcastically expressed his doubt at her marvelous ability to see through him to his "true" feelings. "Now your 'true' angry feelings are coming out at last," she exulted. She had made herself right.

20

Constructive Living Assignments

About Assignments

The essence of assignments is the doing of them, not the reporting or commenting on them in individual sessions. However, we do allow our students to report their accomplishments in individual sessions, because they may need instruction about the methods and meanings of the assignments, and because they deserve our recognition of their efforts. Assignments don't have to be difficult and burdensome. They may be fun to carry out—such as walking, swimming, calling a friend, discovering the flavor of a maple bar. The tougher assignments of CL communicate the instructor's message that the student is ready to handle more difficult tasks.

During one certification training the group of trainees and instructors took a walk up a long road with many side roads and finally arrived at a cliff overlooking a small wooded island. A few days later I assigned one trainee the task of finding that same overlook again on her own. She persevered and succeeded. The next day I gave her the same assignment and asked her to notice how the task was different from the first time she'd performed it. Yet a third time she was given the same assignment. How easy it had become!

When I ask a student to go on silence (such as limiting speech to ten sentences over a period of time), I explain the assignment in terms of its effect on other people. "You use talk to make those around you comfortable and to entertain them, so you talk a lot. With this exercise you will learn that others somehow manage to live their lives even when you are silent." Thus the assignment isn't based on the student's personal need to talk and difficulty keeping quiet. Often an assignment is easier to do when the student sees it as useful to someone else and not merely for his/her self-improvement.

Other assignments and exercises can be found in Constructive Living books, such as *Playing Ball on Running Water* (pp. 105–116), *Even in Summer the Ice Doesn't Melt* (pp. 151–158), *Pools of Lodging for the Moon* (pp. 103–106), *A Thousand Waves* (pp. 125–127), *Thirsty, Swimming in the Lake* (pp. 107–111), *Rainbow Rising from a Stream* (pp. 131–138), and *Plunging through the Clouds* (pp. 25–26).

Magazine Assignments

The following assignments were included in the article about CL in *Claudia* magazine in Brazil.

Give yourself away

Patricia Ryan-Madson, a faculty member at Stanford University, suggests to her Constructive Living students that they give away something every day. A number of other CL instructors, too, work on clearing away the material overload that plagues their lives by offering others items that still have a useful life.

A dating game

Patricia Ryan-Madson also recommends to her students seeking to socialize more that they invite others to go along with them to do ordinary chores such as shopping, laundry, washing the car, and so forth. Such expeditions must be made anyway and don't carry the formality of a date. People deserve to be invited whether they accept the invitation or not.

Give credit where it is due

Gregg Krech suggests that you select your finest accomplishment in life for reflection and recognize the specific contributions made by others that enabled you to accomplish that feat. Similarly, he recommends that you consider the specific support of others you received when you were at your lowest point in life.

Recognize admiration where it is due

Another of Gregg Krech's exercises is to write down the name of the person you admire most. Then write what it is you admire most about that person. You will find that underlying whatever you find admirable about the person is what he or she does, their behavior. In other words, what makes people admirable is what they do. To become admirable people we must do admirable things. The exercise can be extended by interviewing someone else to discover who is their most admired person and the reasons for that esteem.

Setting goals

Dr. Ishu Ishiyama at the University of British Columbia offers the following assignment to his students. Come up with a life goal, then write down what you need to do in the next five years to achieve that goal. Then write down what you can do this year, this month, this week, today.

Embrace criticism

Make a special effort to be accepting of criticism. Find the truth in criticism, the beautiful source that lies beneath it. Don't allow yourself to be so distracted by your hurt or the form the criticism takes that you miss the positive information it contains. The Taoist approach to what appears at first to be a lie is to discover the truth underlying the words. "I never make mistakes" may mean "I dread making mistakes" or "I find it hard to look at my imperfections." Take the same approach to criticism. Similarly, Morita offered this advice about advice—thank the person who offers it, but realize that you have no obligation to follow it. Do the same with criticism.

A New Year's Day activity

On New Year's Day write your epitaph, obituary, and eulogy as you would wish them to be if you were to die during the new year. They should contain an account of your life accomplishments to date and your plans for the coming year. This is a good way to remind yourself of the limited time you have in which to do what needs doing. The same exercise might be repeated on your birthday and the results compared each year. The exercise is not about death itself, but about what you will accomplish before death.

Throw a party

Make the theme of your party a cleanup of the beach or a nearby park. Then provide refreshments and entertainment at the cleaned-up site.

Invite your friends to a quilting bee or some modern equivalent during which you make something to give away to the homeless, a nursing home, a mental institution, or an orphanage. Check with people who have everyday contact with these institutions to find an appropriate purpose for the party.

Throw a gardening party for a convalescing or new neighbor. Invite friends to weed the garden and shrubs and mow the lawn. Then have a barbecue.

Reminders

On a dozen pieces of paper write the question "What is my purpose now?" Post them in various places where you are apt to notice them during the day (e.g., on the phone, the calendar, a doorknob, a file cabinet, the refrigerator, the television). As you come across the notes consider whether you are doing what is necessary to accomplish your purpose. (Suggested by Daniel Hoppe)

Garbage gratitude

Write a letter to the company that collects your trash praising its trash collectors for some specific service they have provided you, such as taking the trash cans out of the enclosure when you forgot to set them by the curb. (Suggested by Daniel Hoppe)

Imperfection

Take ten minutes to write down thirty of your accomplishments, great or small, from anything as simple as eating a sandwich to completing a college degree. Put a check by those things you did perfectly. Notice how many of your accomplishments were achieved even though you did them imperfectly, though you may consider yourself a perfectionist. (Suggested by Rose Anderson)

Take a hike

It will take quite a few steps to work off the calories in one bite of pastry. Why not start walking even before you take a bite? Fred Paterno suggests moving your feet as though you were already on your walk *instead of* taking that bite. By the time he gets to about sixty paces Fred finds his enthusiasm for eating pastries has diminished.

Assignments related to habits

Make something you want to do more convenient to do; make something you don't want to do more inconvenient to do. For example, don't leave sweet snacks readily at hand on the kitchen counter. Keep stationery handy on your desk if you need to write a letter.

Change your morning routine so that it is more efficient or more graceful. Positive changes in habits require attention.

If your consumption of cigarettes (or ice cream or whatever) stays down for a week reward yourself with some other valuable experience; you will have earned it. What you want to aim for is substitution of self-defined "good" habits rather than just stopping the undesirable ones. Otherwise the old ones creep back into the gaps. As is usual CL practice, if you fail, start again from now. A related exercise is to make yourself reward coupons. Each coupon is good for one special activity, like eating a piece of chocolate, or sleeping late one morning, or getting one new software program or CD, or taking a trip, or going for a walk in the woods. Reward yourself with a coupon for completing some difficult or unpleasant task or project.

What do you want to start doing, stop doing, continue doing today? What can you do today to realize a goal for the coming week, month, or year?

For those who wish to lose weight because of their overeating habits, here are some suggestions. Drink a glass of water before meals. Use saucers for your food instead of plates. Leave the serving dishes in the kitchen so that you have to go to the trouble of getting up from the table and walking into it in order to have seconds. Prepare plenty of low-calorie vegetables for every meal, including breakfast. Keep only healthy snacks on hand so that you have to walk to the store for candy or a pastry. Wait at least five minutes before snacking, and have a list of distracting activities available so you may get involved in one and forget about snacking altogether. Keep yourself from growing bored and at home with unhealthy snacks close at hand; get out of the house for a stroll. Don't do grocery shopping when you are hungry. Wash dishes by hand between the main meal and dessert. This practice gives your brain more time to receive and process sensations of fullness from your intestines. Another possible benefit is that dishwashing may distract you from eating more; you might even skip dessert altogether. Save your snack until just before you leave the house so that you aren't tempted to extend the eating.

As always, it is more productive to substitute a behavior than just to stop doing something.

New Perspective Assignments

Perform a service for someone else such as washing the windshield of his/her car. Make a list of the people thanks to whom you are able to do that service. Again, even our kindness to others is a gift from others.

Interview someone who irritates you. Let them do most of the talking. Listen carefully to what they have to say about themselves.

Invite someone you don't know well to lunch.

Find out the birthday of a neighbor or someone at work or school and send that person a handmade birthday card.

Help someone do a chore that they usually do alone.

This assignment is adapted from a Meaningful Life Therapy exercise. "Grinding sesame seeds" has two meanings in Japanese. In addition to the obvious meaning of grinding sesame seeds with a small pestle in a bowl with ridges on the bottom there is the meaning of oiling human relations with flattery. For students who tend to respond negatively and pessimistically we assign the task of pairing off and taking turns talking about the previous day's activities. The listener must find positive things to say about the speaker's activities, even if it requires stretching the remarks to comical extremes. For example, "You cut your finger? How fortunate it wasn't more serious! Your body kindly repairs such wounds for you." Such an exercise is related to the CL advice to seek for the positive source behind all neurotic problems, such as the desire to live longer that underlies my fear of flying.

Taste some food that you don't ordinarily eat.

Go to a public place and make yourself as inconspicuous as possible. Learn through experience the ninja techniques of being unnoticed. Discover the advantages of being socially invisible. What do you see and hear?

Walk silently, leaving no tracks.

Water, Snow, Water

Attention and Memory Assignments

From memory draw a map of a room of your house or apartment. Draw the view from a window of your dwelling. Then check your drawings against reality. What did you leave out? What did you include that was never there or had changed? Notice that the mind often creates colors and forms in memory that may not exist rather than substituting blank spaces for unknown areas.

Select some scene or object for intense observation for ten minutes. Then leave the area and sketch the object of your observation. Return with the sketch and compare what you noticed and remembered with the reality.

Open doors, turn lights on and off, eat, shower, button and unbutton clothing with the opposite hand to that which you are accustomed to using for these activities. Notice the attention this requires.

The assignment to spend at least twenty minutes drawing a single blossom or leaf keeps the attention focused on a single object so that you discover its details. Similarly, find leaves of six different shapes and draw them in detail.

Hot hands is an exercise devised by Ron Madson, a CL instructor in San Francisco. During this exercise done over a period of time one's hands may not be still for more than thirty seconds but must be moving, engaged in some constructive activity.

Hot pants is an extension of the above exercise. People who want more physical exercise may not sit down for more than fifteen minutes at a time. They should carry a timer with them and set it for fifteen minutes every time they sit down.

Discoveries

Find something broken and fix it.
> Find something beautiful and smile at it.
> Find something delicate and protect it.
> Find something ugly and make it look better.

Constructive Living Assignments

Find something dirty and clean it.

Find something weak and make it stronger.

Find something alive and small and observe it and learn from it.

Find something ordinary and make it unusual.

Find something troubled and relieve it.

Find something dark and brighten it.

Find something you don't understand and figure it out.

Find something that looks soft but feels hard.

Find something that looks hard but feels soft.

Find a new use for something that is about to be discarded.

Assignments Related to Speech and Writing

For a period of time all one's sentences must be about oneself, must begin with "I," "My," "In my opinion," "If I were," and so on. For the second period all sentences must omit self-references and deal only with the listener or a third party. Nonreferential statements about objects and the like are also permitted.

Very verbal people's assignment is to limit their speech so that it is sung in short sentences conforming to the four sounds from Beethoven's Fifth: di, di, di, *dum*. Modifying their speech to fit this pattern slows down the speaking, makes it more difficult, and therefore less likely to occur.

An assignment for a person with a great deal of self-focus is to limit speech to ten sentences a day but allow unlimited questions about others.

Ten expressions of thanks and/or ten words of praise are a common daily assignment. Words of praise may indicate recognition of a service well rendered. Such assignments require recognition of what is received from others.

Interview someone you admire. Ask them about who contributed to their success. Ask them about whom *they* admire.

Aim to avoid grumbling, complaining, or criticism for one day. Only praise, thanks, and offers to help are allowed. This assignment is for people who have a great many activities in their lives and usually do them well. They may be dissatisfied with their partners at home or work, partners who seem unable to perform life's tasks as effectively and efficiently as they can. They may feel overburdened and put upon, as carrying more than their share of the load. This assignment turns their attention to the support and contributions rather than the faults and weakness of others.

Write a letter to the editor of a local paper about some community topic. Or write a letter of appreciation to a teacher, a trash collector, a police officer, a store manager, or a relative focusing on what you received from them during this year (or the most recent year you had contact with them).

Write a note of thanks to someone who made it possible for you to be where you are today, *literally.*

Talk only between others' sentences. That is, you may speak one sentence at a time but wait after your own sentence for the other to speak.

Send someone flowers and a thank-you card.

Make a list of what you like about someone. Especially note what it is they do that you find likeable.

Write an application to live for one more year, one more month (adapted from a suggestion made by Simon Bush). What would you promise to do during that period of time?

Make a list of people thanks to whom your ill family member receives medical/social care.

When you do a task, such as making your bed, reflect on the people who have done that same task for you in the past.

Pick a CL maxim that applies to you and use it somehow in your activities during the day.

Clean up your speech. For example, note that the statements "I've had a bad week" and "I am shinky" are inaccurate, in that the generalizations ignore opposite events and behaviors. Be careful not to inflate the use of words like "feel" and "comfortable" and "motivated." The way we speak influences the way we think about the world. Constructive Living recommends the use of artful but realistic speech.

Here are some examples of imprecise speech in need of correction:

> "I'll try to psyche myself up to . . ."
> "(Any motive, but especially a feeling) moved me to . . ."
> "I dealt with my feelings by . . ."
> "These unrecognized feelings . . ."
> "Neurosis is when fear prevents people from doing their job."
> "He was immobilized by fear."
> "(Something) makes me crazy."
> "Until I feel comfortable about it, I can't (any behavior)."
> "I would be willing to . . ."

Can you find the conceptual errors in the above sentences?

Counseling Assignments for Couples

Make a list of at least ten specific qualities of your partner (specific deeds, if possible) that you loved, respected, and admired during courtship days. Next, make a list of at least ten specific qualities (specific deeds, if possible) that you love, respect, and admire about your partner now. Then read off the lists slowly to one another without comment.

Discover something new about your child or your partner and report on it.

Aim to utter ten words of praise and no words of criticism this week.

Find a joint project (painting the garage, volunteer work, cleaning out a closet, taking a trip) to participate in together.

Practice ways to offer criticism to your partner inoffensively (see Chap. 19, "Kind Criticism").

Rather than merely objecting to your partner's ideas, offer alternatives.

Make appointments for further discussion of a topic if one partner wants time out for whatever reason.

Allow a partner who likes neat orderliness to have some personal space that he or she can keep neat and orderly.

As best you can, write a description of one day in the life of your partner as it might be seen through your partner's eyes.

Other Assignments

Nibble at the edge of some large task or objective. For example, if you want more exercise do it during the commercials while watching football on television; or just before shutting down your computer write the first few lines of that long e-mail you owe someone.

When you cry, don't stop everything while crying. Clean your room while you are crying; scrub your tennis shoes while you're crying; feed the birds, take out the trash, weed the garden while you're crying.

Sing to yourself when you are afraid and there is nothing you can do to change the circumstances. (For example, if you are afraid of riding in elevators but must do so.)

Direct a shy child to find another lonely/shy person and help him/her.

Keep a log of feelings; just note the time and what you were feeling. Observe the changes.

Assignments for Specific Students

1. Fear of touching

A once renowned musician telephoned me at the request of one of her friends. She avoids touching people because she feels her energy draining away when she does. She even stays home as much as possible to avoid being touched accidentally. Her boyfriend does shopping and other chores outside the home for her.

I asked her what she is doing for anyone else. What exercise does she get? Is she practicing her musical instrument? Who pays for the treatments that take her out of the home (including massage, fasts, European spas)? Is she working at all? Is she living on her savings?

I offered this woman a free telephone session. However, I told her

that if she wanted another free session she had to carry out the following assignments for any seven consecutive days. Thus she could earn
her next session. Assignments for the first session were:

> To stay out of her house from 9 a.m. to 4 p.m.
> To read a Constructive Living book
> To make something with her own hands for someone else each
> day (cookies, a scrapbook, a tape recording of her music, and
> the like)

The troubled lady asked if making cookies for the residents of
a nearby nursing home or for patients in a local hospital would be
good for her symptoms. I replied that it would certainly be good for
the nursing home residents and hospital patients who received the
cookies. Notice the shift in focus from her situation to the situation
of others. This narrow neurotic self-concern is both the result and the
cause of neurotic suffering.

Assignments for the second session were preceded by praise for
her efforts, "You earned your chance for another session. Congratula-
tions." I didn't ask about whether her symptoms were reduced in order to avoid focusing attention back onto the symptoms at this stage.
Here are the second set of assignments.

> Not to talk about her symptoms to anyone, including her boyfriend
> To continue to stay out of her house from 9 a.m. to 4 p.m.
> To pick up trash in her neighborhood for one hour per day or
> get a part-time job
> To continue creatively making something for someone else each day
> To continue to read Constructive Living books of her choice
> If she were to accidentally brush against someone, even if it was
> the other person's fault, to apologize to that person
> To spend no more than eight hours in bed at night, and take no
> naps during the day
> To list the people thanks to whom she can eat, live in her

apartment, drive, bank, and experience these Constructive Living sessions

2. Post-traumatic panic

A Las Vegas lady was suffering from panic attacks related to a hospital experience months earlier. In the hospital she had had a severe reaction to pain medication following surgery. She had read a Constructive Living book and was trying to keep busy to avoid thinking about the problem, but nausea occasionally interrupted her concentration. The main difficulty occurred when she was first falling asleep. When I asked her about her sleep habits she replied that she went to bed at 10:00 p.m. and got up at 7:00 a.m.

I offered the following advice.

Thank your body for its self-protective response.
Call your difficulty a nausea problem and not a panic attack.
Go to bed at 11 p.m. or later and get up promptly at 7 a.m.; take no naps during the day. Before getting into bed, relax with television or a book or daily CL reflection (what was received from others that day, what she did for others that day, and what troubles she had caused others that day) or some other quiet activity.
Continue to get an appropriate amount of physical activity during the day.
Chew sugarless peppermint gum when the nausea began.

3. A matter of perspective

One young lady calls me to talk about her weakness and misery. I keep pointing out what she has done to work successfully on her problems. She keeps insisting that she is hurting. I acknowledge her communication about the pain and turn her attention to what needs to be done next. I emphasize her strengths and strategies. But she just wants to talk about her failures and hurt.

4. A matter of purpose

Another young lady calls now and then to report the difficulties she's having writing her dissertation. Life brings her many interruptions and successes that interfere with her getting down to it. She prefers to watch television or talk with me about the difficulties rather than actually do the necessary writing. This insightful lady recognizes her avoidance tactics, yet she doesn't change her behavior. I wonder aloud whether the doctorate is really necessary for her. Perhaps she could put it aside for a few years while she explores other areas of her life that are already blossoming. It's up to her.

Her immediate assignment is to keep her television in the closet under some luggage. Then when she wants to watch it she must take it from the closet and set it up. After watching for a maximum of two hours she is to return the television to the closet. Materials for writing the dissertation are to be kept handy. Hopefully, she will find writing less burdensome than having to take out and put away the television set.

5. A matter of possibility

A woman was worrying that she might have suffered a miscarriage. (She was waiting for the test results.) In the meantime she was on an emotional roller coaster, worrying about the effects another miscarriage might have on her mind and body. Her husband wanted to keep trying, but he didn't understand the personal cost to her of doing so. She was wondering what to tell her parents if there had, in fact, been a miscarriage. And she also wondered whether it might perhaps be better to adopt instead. I reminded her that adoption and trying again to produce a child are not mutually exclusive options. She needed to check reality first. If she actually had suffered a miscarriage she could discuss both options for having a child with her husband. Then she could contact her parents with the bad news about the miscarriage and the good news about their decision to adopt. I asked her to keep physically active within the limits of her physician's advice. Sitting around worrying would not be helpful to her mental condition or to her baby. I advised her to make something for her future child, however that child might come into her life. I asked her to avoid talking about her wildly fluctuating feelings of hope, despair, worry, and so forth to business associates or others except as necessary. At the time of this writing the young mother has given birth to a healthy baby boy.

It is not unusual for our worries to be founded on unrealistic imaginings. Checking out reality will not necessarily eliminate worries, but it will give us a more grounded information base for future action.

6. What needs doing?

I cut one individual session short because this particular lady needed to write a paper and wanted to talk about how difficult it was to write papers. Her time would have been better spent working on the paper rather than talking with me.

7. Alcohol and sleep

To the man who wanted to quit his habit of drinking alcohol at bedtime in order to help him sleep I gave the assignment to stay on his feet from 10:00 p.m. until he got into bed—no reading or sex in bed. If he didn't fall asleep within thirty minutes after climbing into bed, he was to get up and do some housework, such as cleaning the kitchen, then go back to bed. Furthermore, he was assigned the task of limiting his alcohol intake to small quantities (so that he would have to go to the store to get more) and storing it in an inconvenient place (e.g., in locked suitcases under other suitcases in the closet).

8. Money talk

To the woman who wanted help in decreasing arguments with her husband over financial matters I assigned the task of making sure that she stated her husband's perspective whenever the subject came up.

Constructive Living Assignments

The goal was to ensure that he would see that she understood his point of view. Then she was to repeat his statements back to him during the argument, both to clarify her understanding of his position and to provide him with a model of proper listening. She was also assigned the task of apologizing to her husband for her habit of throwing objects and stalking out of the house when she was upset. True, being upset is uncontrollable, but it is no excuse for that sort of behavior. Lest the reader think that such assignments are sexist, I would give exactly the same assignments to a husband should he contact me for help with this problem, and, in fact, have done so in other cases.

9. Vague misery

A young man called and said that he was having trouble with "success, failure, and rejection." I know the general meanings of those words, but I had no idea of the experiences and events in his life to which he was affixing those labels. As we talked further, it appeared to me that he was a fellow caught up in abstract talk that pulled him away from everyday reality and was making him miserable. So my initial assignment was that he go through at least one week without using the words "success," "failure," and "rejection." I encouraged him to talk with others about the details of daily experiences and events, but without using those abstractions in the conversations. As much as possible I recommended that he avoid such terms in his thinking for a while as well. He liked the assignment and said he would give it a try.

10. Reality check

A student told me that she wouldn't go for a mammogram because she believes that mammograms cause cancer. Her related assignment was to go to the library and research articles of her choice on mammograms.

21

Constructive Living Tales

Many Mansions

There once, just once, was a very wealthy man who was so pleased with his house and furnishings that he decided to build an exact replica of them in a distant land. That way, if his first house were to be destroyed by fire or storm he would have a completely furnished backup house ready and waiting. Having finished that duplicate house, he decided to build yet another one just in case some unlikely circumstances destroyed the first two. As he was traveling to find a site for the third house he fell over a cliff and died. While so engrossed in worrying and planning for the future he had lost his chance to appreciate the present.

Keeping Score

When the evening newspaper arrives another man carries it to the sofa and props up his cane, always in the same place. He fumbles for his bifocals and opens to the obituary page. World news, sports news, classified ads—all must wait their turn.

"Old Man Trumpe died," he calls out to his wife.

"Well, he lived a good, long life," she murmurs from the kitchen as she washes up the dinner dishes. Table cleaned off, she joins him on the couch.

"Up Piqua way, you know a Hankins?" he asks.

"Maybe Opal's nephew. Heard she had kin in Piqua."

"Harold Hankins. Died in a car accident. Only thirty-two."

"Young. Too young," she sighs respectfully, righteously.

She has sinus "spells," headaches that send her to bed. His legs are becoming useless. Both their fingers are knobby carrots of arthritis. The lines on their faces were etched by Ohio winters until there's no possibility of erasing them.

But this old farm couple are living their lives. They are victors in life's contest. Each day they consult the newspaper scoreboard.

Tennis Tale

"I'll take the intermediate level group," Fred volunteered. He had never taught tennis, for that matter never played it. But he had watched a few matches on television when he was going with a college girl who had a crush on Björn Borg. The beginners probably only needed someone to return the ball to them—he doubted his ability to do that. The advanced level group might catch on to the gaps in his knowledge. But he figured he just might be able to talk himself through a group of intermediates.

"Now I know you want to be able to play tournament tennis. I'm gonna help you do that. The first and guiding principle in tournament tennis is that the pace of the ball is more important than getting it back over the net. You gotta hit it fast to stay in a game. Yeah, I know you've heard the old theme 'Keep the ball in play.' That's all very well for the Saturday games with Aunt Tillie. But you get a guy who serves and volleys, races to the net, and you just punch back a soft return. He'll clobber it. So you got it back over the net. He kills it! Big deal. You lose. It's better to whip that ball back and get it past him even if half the time it goes into the net. You get half the points that way.

"So, everybody, short backswing, fast follow through. Good! Good! Now let's do the backhand. Okay! Fine! Whip it up the line. Whip it crosscourt. Pair off and keep at it. I'll be back in a few minutes."

Fred made quick profits by faking, displaying a fine facade, flaunting it, and fooling others. If his style appeals to you, beware! You've been taking lessons from thousands of Freds in advertising, entertainment, and business.

Some Rocks Don't Roll

"Watch for Falling Rocks" read the sign on the road. One day a rock fell. Actually, it was more of a boulder. It blocked the only road from C.'s house into town. C. tried pushing the boulder off the road, even used the pickup to nudge it, but it was no use. C. then tried drilling and chipping, and even a sledgehammer. All were ineffective. He grew angry and pounded the boulder with his fists, shouting and sobbing in frustration. But the obstacle remained firmly oblivious to C.'s outpouring of emotion. Rocks are maddeningly implacable.

Eventually C. built a detour around the boulder. The bypass was never as smooth and easy to drive on as the original road. It was bumpy, and sometimes it washed out in rainy weather. But boulders are boulders. And C. needed to get to town.

Some rocks are teachers. Teaching rocks are the ones that students notice. C.'s rock was a teacher.

Traversing the Wall

There is an effective way to cross a certain sheer cliff face. Over hundreds of years a kind of path has been worn into the rock by the feet of countless climbers. Due to geologic shifts and the inclinations of trekkers, one can find a variety of side paths paralleling the deepest indentations in the rock. One embarks on a new course across the cliff face at some risk. Not a few have fallen as they sought a new path to their destination. Those whose attention drifted, those who found themselves distracted from the careful placement of their hands and feet, could expect slips and startled moments and possibly disaster. Even the clearest path is not without its dangers.

Wise adventurers use the best equipment available to them. They train themselves for the passage. They use all their senses to make the crossing safely.

Not only do they enjoy satisfaction when they have traversed the cliff face safely, but they experience an acute vitality during the crossing itself. Almost anyone can slog through a marshy meadow. Moving through the heights is quite another thing.

The Ugly Spouseling

Once upon a dissatisfying time a woman married a man who grew uglier and uglier as the years passed. Partly he just became ugly naturally; partly his self-grooming was to blame. The woman went around complaining about her husband to anyone who would listen. She criticized him when he was present and when he was absent. She went to the length of buying advertising space in her local newspaper and publishing his picture along with her complaints about his terrible looks.

What do you suppose she was trying to accomplish by all this grumbling? Do you think she had found an effective way of changing her husband? What tactics might have proven more successful?

Fall Guys

Two junior-high-school kids new to Mrs. T.'s English class sit talking to each other while the teacher tries to get their attention. Finally, Mrs. T. can bear their indifference to the lesson no longer.

"Billy! Suzy!"

"Would you please keep it down, Mrs. T.?" Billy grins insolently. "It's hard for us to talk with you making all that noise."

"Perhaps you two would like to continue your conversation in the hall," Mrs. T. responds.

"Sounds like a great idea." Billy is always ready with a quick rejoinder.

The two students move their chairs into the hall to the cheers of their classmates. Billy and Suzy believe that they are heroes.

They are certainly appreciated by their knowledgeable classmates, but not in the way they think. Soon they hear the sounds of a class-room party. Mrs. T. is passing out soft drinks and popcorn. The class plays spelling games. Laughter reaches the hall as Billy and Suzy's glee turns to surprised understanding. In Mrs. T.'s class, being sent out into the hall (often, but not always) is the signal for celebration for the rest of the class. Life turns out as it turns out.

Mirrors

Once upon a time there was a beautiful woman who said that she didn't want jewels, she wanted stones. But what she really wanted was mirrors. She met a man who had stones, but he couldn't polish his stones to make them into mirrors. He tried to explain about his rough stones, but his language was limited.

Fortunately, all stones and all people are already mirrors. But many of them don't know it.

The Rebel Princess

Once upon an affluent time a princess was born to a minor king in the land of the North. She grew up in wealth, always wondering why she was so blessed and what she could do to earn the privileges that birth had afforded her. She rebelled against her high position, undertaking all sorts of difficult courses and trials and occupations in order to prove to herself that she deserved what she had. She felt at ease only when she was out trekking in nature, because nature didn't seem to care that she was a princess.

As she grew older she gradually realized that no one earned what he/she had, that we all receive more than we deserve. That under-standing brought her a sigh of relief and the determination to contin-ue the satisfying task of working on her natural attempts to repay her ordinary, human debt.

"It's okay," she said, "everyone is nobility."

A Gift of Nice

Once upon a time there was a charming young lady living in the fictional land of Southern Califodonia. She tried very hard not to criticize others, to be thoughtful, to be generally nice. She learned that if she kept a low profile and didn't cause much trouble to others she could get by in life fairly easily. She was very careful. She tried to think and act slowly so she would make the fewest mistakes possible and cause minimal trouble and hide her imperfections. As the years passed she began to feel trapped in a kind of box she had built around herself. She knew that she was very skillful at some aspects of life, but by now she half believed some of the modest, humble things she said about herself.

She had tried so hard to be the kind of person who deserved a good life. Then she heard that no one could earn a good life, that a good life is a gift, that even being thoughtful and careful and nice are all gifts. So confidence in her ability to change and grow would be a gift, too. How kind of Reality! Now she had a new reason for being the best kind of person she could be.

Fielding Techniques

Once upon a time there was a clever young man living north of the Usapotamia border.

He had learned (perhaps at home, perhaps at college) that whenever he was challenged or questioned he could throw lots of words at the questioner and get pretty good results. If the words sounded authoritative, scientific, or medical the results were even better. If the words were about his own personal experience no one could challenge them. His solution was much better than curling up and lying down submissively when questioned or challenged. Sometimes he slanted his words just a wee bit to make his point.

As he grew older he stumbled upon another alternative response to questions and challenges and tried it on for size. The alternative involved trying to figure out the needs of the questioner who was asking the question. Then his response was to give a reply as a kind of gift that met the needs that lay behind the question. It was a bit harder to do, and he couldn't always defend his original position when focusing on the needs of the other person. But he was pretty tough and could handle vulnerability by the time he learned about this kind of response. He was pleased with the new tactic, and he found that the people around him were pleased, too.

Fairy-tale Accommodations

Once upon a time people lived in fairy tales. One popular fairy-tale apartment building was called a Siggy. It was basically of German-Austrian construction, with elaborate towers and a very, very deep basement. The structure itself had grown old and its architectural faults increasingly apparent. Nevertheless, however rickety a dwelling it was, some people preferred its familiarity to the inconvenience of moving to a better-built fairy tale. Siggy buildings had wealthy landlords. The apartments were prominently located in the finer sections of their cities. Some management groups made efforts to remodel them, but the results were only cosmetic. Tenants endured everyday inconveniences and focused on the buildings cultured past. Rents remained quite high.

Other fairy-tale structures had steeples or ivy-covered walls or official facades of various sorts. They attracted quite a few folks. Rare individuals built elaborate structures of greenback plants. People in those days had quite active imaginations. Many of them appear to have forgotten that, however reassuring, all fairy tales have endings, even psychoanalytic ones.

Rings

Two people are standing on a platform high above the ground. A pair of trapeze rings hang suspended just out of reach from the platform.

The couple must somehow work together to grab the rings and swing to the platform of their dreams across the way. At last they discover that if one stands on the shoulders of the other, they can fall forward off the platform and one member of the pair can just reach the rings. Then they can swing themselves to the next platform. They have a certain degree of faith that one of them can grab the rings before they both plunge to their deaths.

On nearby platforms stand whole groups of people. There are no rings to help them get to their platforms of prosperity. They must learn to balance themselves one on top of the other, then topple the whole column of balancing humans with the goal of enabling one member of the group to grab onto the far platform as the others fall. At first, only the person on top can be saved by grasping the far platform, as he loses hold of those beneath him. But this restricts his ability to move on to even higher platforms, so those lower down the column are unjustly sacrificed. Eventually groups learn to hold on to one another as they are falling so that the person on top can pull the others up onto the far platforms too.

The G Spot

Once upon a time there was a skillful dancer, Vern, who performed at a number of clubs, including one called The G Spot. This dancer sometimes wondered if he was fully qualified to do all these performances. For the most part he was self-taught. Whenever he met someone new he would insist on dancing for that person to check out whether his new acquaintance could see through his performance to the imperfection behind it. He was so pleased whenever someone appreciated his dancing. After all, through it he wanted to provide a good service. It was something he could give to others. However, sometimes he wondered if he deserved his audiences.

One day a dancing group came to town. At The G Spot they all sat down for a drink of iced tea and began to talk. Vern joined in their conversation, though he sometimes got up to do a little dance for them, it had become such a habit. The dancers were talking about how they all sometimes thought they weren't dancing as well as they should, that they were worried others would see through their imperfect performances, and that they sometimes doubted their ability to keep the show going.

"Wow!" thought Vern (and then he did a little dance about this discovery). "Everyone else is like me. Or, rather, I am like everyone else. They all sometimes think they are in over their heads, that their faults will be discovered, that the music is going too fast for their dancing abilities. Probably even the members of my audiences are like that, too."

Vern was so relieved to make this discovery that from that day on he danced even better, more joyfully—and less often. (This tale, too, is a kind of dance.)

Second-string Guru

After a few moments of casual conversation the guru faced him squarely.

"You are protected by politeness," the guru observed.

"Yes, like the Japanese," he replied.

"Yes, I see it."

"And *you* are protected by holiness," he remarked.

The guru paused for a moment, "Yes, that is so. You see that aspect well."

It was a cautious answer. Clever gurus don't let you live alongside them twenty-four hours a day.

Assassins Anonymous

It was a meeting of the local Assassins Anonymous chapter. Terrorists, hit people, and killers of all sorts sat in a circle discussing the psychological twists and turns and dead ends that had led to their tragic trade. The week before they had explored the high that came from "claiming" responsibility for an act of violence rather than "admitting" responsibility for such an act. How the press fed into their tangled needs. How much they wanted to be admired and loved like anyone else—some "because of" and some "in spite of" their deadly actions.

This week a masked member held the center of attention. Much effort had been expended on encouraging the person in the hot seat to remove that mask, but to no avail.

"When I was caught and tried for the murders I lied under oath. Of course I lied. I wanted to save my skin. Anyone would have lied. Or so I thought. Lately I've been thinking that if my oath isn't dependable, if I can lie so easily under oath, then I can lie to anyone, even to myself. I can't trust me. Who am I if I can't expect myself to answer any question honestly with the best knowledge I have? I sold my soul to save my skin."

So they continued to discuss the masked killer's problem well into the night. The group sought to find resolution in words and reframing and childhood abuse. They comforted and empathized and supported. They carefully ignored the dripping blood of their victims and the empty nights of the survivors. They avoided discussing the savage selfishness of the killings. They sought healing of a pseudo wound. They pursued firm footing in clouds.

Whatever one might say under oath, everyone knows that there are no bargain prices on the soul.

The Sinking Islands

Once upon an affluent time some island people went flying around the world carrying cameras and buying brand-name goods. They brought back suitcases full of foreign goods purchased inexpensively in foreign countries. They threw away the clothes and television sets and furniture they had bought last year in order to make room for this year's purchases.

Little by little their island began to sink under the load of imports and trash. The rate of sinking was so slow as to be hardly perceptible. Nevertheless, the people began to worry: What will happen in the long run? What will happen to our grandchildren? Nonetheless, they weren't about to give up importing foreign goods, and they had no plans to stop throwing away huge amounts of outdated items.

Some politicians suggested that they float their islands on money. Others suggested that they export their outdated goods to Southeast Asian countries and so lighten the burden on the islands. Young people suggested that if the heavy burdens of responsibility were lightened the islands would not sink. But it was these very young people who were doing most of the traveling, buying, and discarding. If travel agents could just keep most of the population on airplanes at any given time much of the weight would be relieved.

What to do? What to do?

22

Constructive Living Maxims

Maxims from the Author

You're not as old as you feel. You're only as old as you are!

Another birthday! How kind of reality to keep bringing them to us!

You don't check your watch when you're laughing.

You find out most about the path by traveling on it.

CL is thanksdoing.

Illness makes the heart go ponder.

CL—Just the way it is.

Maxims from CL Instructors and Students

Do until you're done (dead); give until you're gone. (Sue Cole)

Recipe for Constructive Living: Take self. Separate into gifts.
   Serve imperfectly. (Paul Kroner)

Behave yourself. (Margaret Moenich)

Gratitude comes and gratitude goes,/What needs doing is under
   your nose. (Margaret Moenich)

Doing, doing, done. (Trudy Boyl, Gottfried Miterreger, and
   David Hubbard)

Wake up and thank the coffee. (Holiday Temple Jackson)

It's never too late to be on time. (Holiday Temple Jackson)

The present is a present. (James Guswiler)

Shinky neurotics—Ready . . . Aim . . . Aim . . . Aim . . . .
   (David Chapman)

23

Constructive Living Poem

Compared with death, neurosis is insignificant.
No living person knows what death is—except that it is a word.
So death is a meaningless standard.
Purposes have meaning. They are meaningful standards.
It is useful to fit behavior to purposes.
Words have only word reality.
This pen is not a "pen."
This purpose is not "writing."
There is just this.
So CL theory is just a kind of word graphic of reality.
Don't be fooled by it.
Hold to reality.

Postscript—Healing America

Don't get me wrong. This is a great country. I remember tears coming to my eyes as I reentered Immigration at LAX and the officer said "Welcome home." I travel to Japan twice each year where I lecture in Japanese to Japanese people about Japanese psychotherapies. But America is my home. Of course, it is not a perfect home. This book is my attempt to encourage Americans to make this country even better than it is today. The critical problems I have addressed here are the extremes of (1) self-focus and (2) feeling focus.

Americans were not always overwhelmed by these unrealistic and impractical values, as we shall see. We bought into them because supposed experts in mental health proclaimed them as the healthy way to go. Suffering people who went into therapy were taught to focus on themselves and their feelings. For many years professionals believed (wrongly) that exclusive emphasis on self and feelings would actually help people overcome neurosis, post-traumatic stress disorder, and other miseries. Talking about themselves and their emotions was supposed to heal clients. Here I have offered an alternative perspective and an alternative strategy for dealing with human misery that is easy to understand, practical, useful, and realistic, though sometimes hard to practice consistently. I invite you to reconsider what many of you readers have taken for granted about "the pursuit of happiness."

Our Constitution guarantees us the right to "the *pursuit* of happiness." The founding fathers were sharp enough to realize that no one can guarantee the right to happiness. Happiness is a feeling; it comes and goes. The *pursuit* of happiness is behavior; it is what people do in the hope of achieving happiness. The doing, the behavior, is a guaranteed right that may or may not result in happiness. This important difference between feelings (what happens to us) and behavior (what we do) must be kept in mind or we are likely to direct our efforts in unrealistic directions.

Consider the pioneers who pulled handcarts and wagons across the Great Plains of the western United States. Imagine them drawing their covered wagons into a circle and sharing long talks about their feelings. Imagine their taking the time to get to the bottom of their feelings of fear and uncertainty while their wagons sat idly by. Such absurdity doesn't fit historical reality. What actually happened was that the pioneers, while feeling fear and hope and doubts and a range of other feelings, KEPT MOVING THEIR WAGONS WEST.

You understand.

For more information about Constructive Living, go to the websites at constructiveliving.org; www.constructiveliving2.weebly.com; constructiveliving.com; and others.

References

Berkowitz, Leonard. "The Case for Bottling up Rage." *Psychology Today* (July 1973): 24–31.

Cleary, Thomas, ed. *Timeless Spring.* Tokyo: Weatherhill, 1980.

Edelman, Marian. *The Measure of Our Success.* Boston: Beacon Press, 1993.

Shimomura, Torataro. "D. T. Suzuki's Place in the History of Human Thought." In Masao Abe, ed., *A Zen Life: D. T. Suzuki Remembered.* New York: Weatherhill, 1986.

By the author

Reynolds, David K. 1976. *Morita Psychotherapy.* Berkeley: University of California Press.

———. 1977. "Morita Therapy in America." In T. Kora and K. Ohara, eds. *Modern Morita Therapy.* Tokyo: Hakuyosha.

———. 1977. "Naikan Therapy: An Experiential View." *International Journal of Social Psychiatry* 23, no. 4: 252–264.

———. 1979. "Psychodynamic Insight and Morita Psychotherapy." *Japanese Journal of Psychotherapy Research* 5, no. 4: 58–60.

———. 1980. *The Quiet Therapies.* Honolulu: University Press of Hawai'i.

———. 1981. "Morita Psychotherapy." In R. Corsini, ed., *Handbook of Innovative Psychotherapies.* New York: Wiley.

———. 1981. "Naikan Therapy." In R. Corsini, ed., *Handbook of Innovative Psychotherapies.* New York: Wiley.

———. 1981. "Psychocultural Perspectives on Death." In P. Ahmed, ed., *Living and Dying with Cancer.* New York: Elsevier.

———. 1983. *Naikan Psychotherapy: Meditation for Self-Development.* Chicago: University of Chicago Press.

——— . 1984. *Constructive Living.* Honolulu: University of Hawai'i Press.

——— . 1984. *Living Lessons.* Tokyo: Asahi Shuppansha.

——— . 1984. *Playing Ball on Running Water.* New York: Morrow.

——— . 1986. *Even in Summer the Ice Doesn't Melt.* New York: Morrow.

——— . 1987. "Japanese Models of Psychotherapy." In E. Norbeck and M. Lock, eds., *Health, Illness, and Medical Care in Japan.* Honolulu: University of Hawai'i Press.

——— . 1987. "Morita Therapy in America." In K. Ohara, ed., *Morita Therapy: Theory and Practice.* Tokyo: Kongen (in Japanese).

——— . 1988. *Constructive Living for Young People.* Tokyo: Asahi.

——— , ed. 1989. *Flowing Bridges, Quiet Waters.* Albany: SUNY Press.

——— . 1989. "Meaningful Life Therapy." *Culture, Medicine and Psychiatry* 13: 457–463.

——— . 1989. "On Being Natural: Two Japanese Approaches to Healing." In A. A. Sheikh and K. S. Sheikh, eds., *Eastern and Western Approaches to Healing.* New York: Wiley.

——— . 1989. *Pools of Lodging for the Moon.* New York: Morrow.

——— . 1990. *A Thousand Waves.* New York: Morrow.

——— . 1991. *Thirsty, Swimming in the Lake.* New York: Morrow.

——— , ed. 1992. *Plunging through the Clouds.* Albany: SUNY Press.

——— . 1992. *Rainbow Rising from a Stream.* New York: Morrow.

——— . 1993. *Reflections on the Tao te Ching.* New York: Morrow.

——— . 2002. *A Handbook for Constructive Living.* New York: Morrow, 1995; Honolulu: University of Hawai'i Press.

——— , and C. W. Kiefer. 1977. "Cultural Adaptability as an Attribute of Therapies: The Case of Morita Psychotherapy." *Culture, Medicine, and Psychiatry* 1: 395–412.

——— , and Joe Yamamoto. 1973. "Morita Psychotherapy in Japan." In Jules Masserman, ed., *Current Psychiatric Therapies* 13: 219–227.

Production Notes for…

Reynolds / *Water, Snow, Water*
Cover design by Julie Matsuo-Chun
Text design and composition by
Julie Matsuo-Chun with display type in
Univers and text type in Minion Pro
Printing and binding by Edwards Brothers Malloy
Printed on 55# EBM Blue White, 360ppi